RIVULETS OF PROSE

CRITICAL ESSAYS

BY

WALT WHITMAN

Edited by CAROLYN WELLS &
ALFRED F. GOLDSMITH

Essay Index Reprint Series

BOOKS FOR LIBRARIES PRESS

FREEPORT, NEW YORK

First Published 1928
Reprinted 1969

STANDARD BOOK NUMBER:
8369-1163-6

LIBRARY OF CONGRESS CATALOG CARD NUMBER:
78-88037

PRINTED IN THE UNITED STATES OF AMERICA

RIVULETS OF PROSE

A hitherto unpublished portrait, reproduced from an early
daguerrotype, now in Walt Whitman's House Collection,
Camden, New Jersey

With Affection
TO RAY S. GOLDSMITH
For Her Sympathetic Assistance

FOREWORD

NINE out of ten readers would acclaim Walt Whitman a one-book man. But the tenth would demur at this characterization. While *Leaves of Grass* is well known to the many, Whitman's prose work is known to the few.

To be sure, the prose has not the same appeal as the poems, but as part and parcel of the author's work it should be given its rightful place, which, in general, is not done.

Leaves of Grass is Whitman's lifework, his life, himself. It was written and rewritten and polished, and then left unfinished, with the same final despair that Da Vinci left Mona Lisa's smile.

But Whitman's prose, at least the greater part of it, is effortlessly written, and seldom revised or amended. The prose, in almost every instance, is for the matter only, never for the manner.

Of the *Leaves*, the poet says: "No one will get

at my verses who insists on viewing them as a
literary performance, or attempt at such performance."

This is even truer of the prose writings. They
are far from a literary performance, or an attempt at such, but they have their place among
the author's works, and should be recognized and
read by every student of the poet.

There is much of the prose, so much in fact,
that it is neglected because of its very volume.
A great deal of it is autobiographical, and this,
intelligently read, gives us Whitman from an
objective viewpoint. *Leaves of Grass* is too subjective to reveal his whole character; it needs the
complement of his prose to give us the complete
individual.

Leaves of Grass has been called a portrait of
the man. It is more than that; it is a mirror. But
the prose *is* a portrait. In *Leaves of Grass,* the
author thinks, talks, writes only of himself. In
the prose he turns to others, and from that we
get a broader view, a truer relative proportion.

He says himself, the war brought him out,
made him, and his prose about the war gives us

pictures of him which *Leaves of Grass* only hints at.

The war found him already in the throes of creation of his great work, already in the fight for its existence and recognition, already three editions accomplished and more in preparation. But he found time for his war work and his prose writings about it, these forming biography of those troublous times.

In the prose we lose sight of much of his vanity and egoism. We get at the human side more prosaically and less subtly than it is set forth in the poems.

Self-glorification and bombast are less noticeable, and the more lovable, if less exalted self is in evidence.

Whitman had the patience of Job and the perseverance of Bruce's spider. His one unswerving determination was to get his great book accepted, unexpurgated and untampered with. He was indifferent to criticism, though avid of praise.

Meantime, he wrote his prose. In collection it fills five hundred closely typed pages. Much of it is negligible, except as it reveals the man himself.

The mirror of *Leaves of Grass* cannot give us the real man as the portraiture of the prose does.

To quote from an essay by Leon H. Vincent:

"From the prose writings we learn in a few pages how simple-minded, patient and lovable this man really was; how reverent of genius, how free from envy, undisturbed by suffering, ill repute and delayed hopes. There was something at once pathetic and noble in his patience, in his magnificent repose and stability. The impersonal character of the tree and the rock, which he admired so much, became in a measure his. He bided his time. The success of other poets awakened no jealousy. He never called names, never picked flaws in the work of his brother bards. The better we know him the more dignified and lofty his figure becomes."

And this better knowing of him comes from the study of his prose writings. He has been called the best loved and the best hated of modern poets, but small mention is made of him as a prose writer.

Yet, though his prose may not be regarded

FOREWORD

with the approval given to his poems, it should be familiar to his readers, if only for the side lights it gives on the man's personality.

In this volume, we have endeavored to keep in a small compass, and confined to one general subject, the comments, criticisms and opinions of Walt Whitman regarding men and books.

The selections here presented are, many of them, taken from books long out of print and not readily available. Some of them were printed anonymously or over an assumed name.

Some appeared first in newspapers and periodicals; they were often edited or revised by Whitman before being printed in book form, in Specimen Days, November Boughs, Good Bye My Fancy and the Complete Prose.

Use has not been made of the various prefaces and introductions to the different editions of *Leaves of Grass*, interesting though they are. These and the long autobiographical essays cover too large and widespread a field. We are limited to the actual opinions of Whitman regarding men and letters.

John Bailey, a wise and just commentator, deplores the fact that Whitman's executors saw fit to reprint what he calls ignorant exuberances dug out of old newspaper articles. He opines that they only block the way to an appreciation of the great achievements of his genius when it was engaged in its proper work.

But we view the situation differently, and hold that in spite of certain crudities and banalities these papers help to show forth the man and his times, and we claim interest for them, more because they are the work of their author, than because of their inherent value.

In the "Uncollected Poetry and Prose of Walt Whitman" edited by Prof. Emory Holloway, are many book reviews and short articles that show the critical ability of Whitman in his early newspaper work.

John Burroughs, faithful friend of Whitman, calls him an unbookish spirit and says his is the voice of a man and not of a scholar.

Burroughs says also, of Whitman's writings: "It is the literary and poetic value alone that can save them. Their philosophy, their democracy, their vehement patriotism, their religious ardor,

FOREWORD

their spirit of comradeship, or what not, will not alone suffice. All depends upon the manner in which these things are presented to us. Do we get the reality or words about the reality? No matter what the content, unless into the whole is breathed the breath of the true creative artist they will surely perish. Oblivion awaits every utterance not touched with the life of the spirit."

Whitman's prose has not sunk into oblivion except in so far as it has been neglected by compilers or publishers, and it is the intent of this volume to bring to the attention of students of Walt Whitman the views he held about others besides himself.

Aside from his comments and criticisms of others, Whitman occasionally commented on his own work, usually anonymously. One of the most important instances is "Walt Whitman and His Poems" an anonymous review by Whitman of *Leaves of Grass* and its significance. This was first published in the United States Review in 1855. It was then inserted among the press notices which were included in the second issue of the first edition of *Leaves of Grass,* Brooklyn 1855. This review was also reprinted in "Imprints" 1860, and again published in "In Re Walt Whitman" 1893 over Whitman's own name.

Perhaps authors of to-day are not quite in a position to decry these innocent methods of self advertisement. As yet, Whitman had no publisher to look after these matters for him.

And it must be admitted that he fired a shot heard round the world, when he calmly used a signed line from Emerson's letter on the back of his new volume. That was a consummate example of his *Me Imperturbe* attitude.

The *Boz and Democracy* article was very early work, published in Brother Jonathan, in February, 1842. Yet it is better, in many ways, than some of his later prose writings.

We know that his comments and criticisms were, for the most part, hurriedly written, and printed without revision, but so much the more, perhaps, do they show forth the spontaneous ideas of the man, and his first-hand judgment of his fellow men.

FOREWORD

Yet, we are not presenting these prose selections as masterpieces, or indeed, with any question of their merit or value from a literary standpoint.

We offer them as Walt Whitman's opinions and comments, and as such they carry their own right to attention. For no student of Whitman can afford to be ignorant of this side of his genius, and reading his prose will stimulate and broaden the interest that is so rapidly growing in all the works of the poet.

Perhaps Whitman's greatest limitations were a lack of a sense of humor and a lack of schooling. Also, against him is charged colossal vanity and egotism.

But against these there is a mountain of fine qualities to be catalogued.

No better word-portrait was ever penned than John Burroughs gives on the first page of his book about Whitman.

"I call this place Whitman land, because in many ways it is typical of my poet—an amphitheater of precipitous rock, slightly veiled with a delicate growth of verdure, enclosing a few acres of prairie-like land,

once the site of an ancient lake, now a garden of unknown depth and fertility. Elemental ruggedness,
savageness and grandeur, combined with a wonderful
tenderness, modernness and geniality. There rise the
gray-scarred cliffs, crowned here and there with a
dead hemlock or pine, where, morning after morning,
I have seen the bald eagle perch and here at their feet
this level area of tender humus, with three perennial
springs of delicious cold water flowing in its margin;
a huge granite bowl filled with the elements and po-
tencies of life. . . . This scene and situation, so
primitive and secluded, yet so touched with and
adapted to civilization, responding to the moods of
both sides of the life of imagination of a modern
man, seems, I repeat, typical in many ways of my
poet, and is a veritable Whitman land. Whitman does
not to me suggest the wild and unkempt as he seems
to do to many; he suggests the cosmic and the elemental, and this is one of the dominant thoughts that
run through my dissertation. Scenes of power and
savagery in nature were more welcome to him, probably more stimulating to him, than the scenes of the
pretty and placid, and he cherished the hope that he
had put into his work some of the tonic and fortify-
ing quality of Nature in her more grand and primitive aspects. His wildness is only the wildness of the
great primary forces from which we draw our health
and strength. Underneath all his looseness, or free

launching forth of himself, is the sanity and repose of nature."

Another commentator says that Whitman is always either idolized or derided.

The idolators are coming to the fore at present. It would be difficult to name an author who has had more enraptured praises or more sincere and genuine friends, both among his contemporaries and those who know him by his work alone.

His friend Thomas Harned said, "I want no other God than Walt Whitman; I want no other Bible than *Leaves of Grass.*"

In a recent essay, Christopher Morley declares: "I can only conjecture that the 1855 Preface sank from sight because it was so astoundingly beautiful."

Few have been more written about whether in full biographies or shorter essays.

Among the earliest and best is Bliss Perry's *Walt Whitman* and in it we find a prophetic utterance already coming true.

"No Whitman myth, favorable or unfavorable, can forever withstand the accumulated evidence as to

Whitman's actual character. Not in vain was he photographed, reported, advertised, Boswellized. The wild buffalo strength myth, which he himself loved to cultivate, has gone; the Sir Galahad myth, so touchingly cherished by O'Connor, has gone, too; and Dr. Bucke's myth is fast going. We have in their place something very much better; a man earthy, incoherent, arrogant, but elemental and alive."

A man who said, truly,

"A thousand warbling echoes have started to life within me, never to die."

And whose own beautiful threnody might be his line,

"Lilac and star bird
Twined with the chant of my soul."
CAROLYN WELLS
ALFRED F. GOLDSMITH

CONTENTS

RIVULETS OF PROSE

WALT WHITMAN AND HIS POEMS

An anonymous review, by Whitman, of Leaves of Grass.
This was first published in "The United States Review"
(September, 1855) *and then inserted among the press
notices which prefaced the first edition (2nd issue) of*
Leaves of Grass (*Brooklyn,* 1855).

AN American bard at last! One of the roughs,
large, proud, affectionate, eating, drinking, and
breeding, his costume manly and free, his face
sunburnt and bearded, his posture strong and
erect, his voice bringing hope and prophecy to
the generous races of young and old. We shall
cease shamming and be what we really are. We
shall start an athletic and defiant literature. We
realize now how it is, and what was most lacking. The interior American republic shall also
be declared free and independent.

For all our intellectual people, followed by
their books, poems, novels, essays, editorials, lectures, tuitions and criticisms, dress by London

and Paris modes, receive what is received there, obey the authorities, settle disputes by the old tests, keep out of rain and sun, retreat to the shelter of houses and schools, trim their hair, shave, touch not the earth barefoot, and enter not the sea except in a complete bathing dress. One sees unmistakably genteel persons, traveled, college-learned, used to be served by servants, conversing without heat or vulgarity, supported on chairs, or walking through handsomely carpeted parlors, or along shelves bearing well-bound volumes, and walls adorned with curtained and collared portraits, and china things, and nick-nacks. But where in American literature is the first show of America? Where are the gristle and beards, and broad breasts, and space and ruggedness and nonchalance that the souls of the people love? Where is the tremendous outdoors of these states? Where is the majesty of the federal mother, seated with more than antique grace, calm, just, indulgent to her brood of children, calling them around her, regarding the little and the large and the younger and the older with perfect impartiality? Where is the vehement growth of our cities? Where is the spirit of the strong rich life of the American mechanic, farmer, sailor, hunter, and miner? Where is the huge composite of all other nations, cast in a fresher and brawnier matrix, passing adolescence, and needed this day live and arrogant to lead the marches of the world?

Self-reliant, with haughty eyes, assuming to himself all the attributes of his country, steps Walt Whitman into literature, talking like a man unaware that there was ever hitherto such a production as a book, or such a being as a writer. Every move of him has the free play of the muscle of one who never knew what it was to feel that he stood in presence of a superior. Every word that falls from his mouth shows silent disdain and defiance of the old theories and forms. Every phrase announces new laws; not once do his lips unclose except in conformity with them. With light and rapid touch he first indicates in prose the principles of the foundation of a race of poets so deeply to spring from the American people, and become ingrained through them, that their Presidents shall not be

the common referees so much as that great race
of poets shall. He proceeds himself to exemplify
this new school, and set models for their expression and range of subjects. He makes audacious
and native use of his own body and soul. He must
re-create poetry with the elements always at
hand. He must imbue it with himself as he is,
disorderly, fleshy, and sensual, a lover of things,
yet a lover of men and women above the whole
of the other objects of the universe. His work is
to be achieved by unusual methods. Neither
classic or romantic is he, nor a materialist any
more than a spiritualist. Not a whisper comes out
of him of the old stock talk and rhyme of poetry
—not the first recognition of gods or goddesses,
or Greece or Rome. No breath of Europe, or her
monarchies or priestly conventions, or her notions of gentlemen and ladies founded on the
idea of caste, seems ever to have fanned his face
or been inhaled into his lungs. But in their stead
pour vast and fluid the fresh mentality of this
mighty age, and the realities of this mighty continent, and the sciences and discoveries of the
present world. Not geology, nor mathematics,

[4]

nor chemistry, nor navigation, nor astronomy, nor anatomy, nor phrenology, nor engineering, is more true to itself than Walt Whitman is true to them. They and the other sciences underlie his whole superstructure. In the beauty of the work of the poet, he affirms, are the tuft and final applause of science.

Affairs then are this man's poems. He will still inject nature through civilization. The movement of his verses is the sweeping movement of great currents of living people, with a general government and state and municipal governments, courts, commerce, manufactures, arsenals, steamships, railroads, telegraphs, cities with paved streets, and aqueducts and police and gas—myriads of travelers arriving and departing—newspapers, elections, and all the features and processes of the nineteenth century in the wholesomest race and the only stable forms of politics at present upon the earth. Along his words spread the broad impartialities of the United States. No innovations must be permitted on the stern severities of our liberty and equality. Undecked also is this poet with senti-

mentalism, or jingle, or nice conceits of flowery
similes. He appears in his poems surrounded by
women and children, and by young men, and by
common objects and qualities. He gives to each
just what belongs to it, neither more nor less.
That person nearest him, that person he ushers
hand in hand with himself. Duly take places in
his flowing procession, and step to the sounds of
the newer and larger music, the essences of
American things, and past and present events—
the enormous diversity of temperature and agriculture and mines—the tribes of red aborigines
—the weatherbeaten vessels entering new ports,
or making landings on rocky coasts—the first
settlements north and south—the rapid stature
and impatience of outside control—the sturdy
defiance of '76, and the war and peace, and the
leadership of Washington, and the formation of
the Constitution—the Union always surrounded
by blatherers and always calm and impregnable
—the perpetual coming of immigrants—the
wharf-hemmed cities and superior marine—the
unsurveyed interior—the loghouses and clear-

ings and wild animals and hunters and trappers
—the fisheries and whaling and gold-digging—
the endless gestation of new states—the conven-
ing of Congress every December, the members
coming up from all climates, and from the utmost parts—the noble character of the free
American workman and workwoman—the
fierceness of the people when well-roused—the
ardor of their friendships—the large amative-
ness—the equality of the female with the male—
the Yankee swap—the New York firemen and
the target excursion—the southern plantation
life—the character of the northeast and of the
northwest and southwest—and the character of
America and the American people everywhere.
For these the old usages of poets afford Walt
Whitman no means sufficiently fit and free, and
he rejects the old usages. The style of the bard
that is waited for is to be transcendent and new.
It is to be indirect and not direct or descriptive
or epic. Its quality is to go through these to much
more. Let the age and wars (he says) of other
nations be chanted, and their eras and charac-

ters be illustrated, and that finish the verse. Not so (he continues) the great psalm of the republic. Here the theme is creative and has vista. Here comes one among the well-beloved stone-cutters, and announces himself, and plans with decision and science, and sees the solid and beautiful forms of the future where there are now no solid forms.

The style of these poems, therefore, is simply their own style, new-born and red. Nature may have given the hint to the author of the "Leaves of Grass," but there exists no book or fragment of a book which can have given the hint to them. All beauty, he says, comes from beautiful blood and a beautiful brain. His rhythm and uniformity he will conceal in the roots of his verses, not to be seen of themselves, but to break forth loosely as lilacs on a bush, and take shapes compact as the shapes of melons or chestnuts or pears.

The poems of the "Leaves of Grass" are twelve in number. Walt Whitman at first proceeds to put his own body and soul into the new versification:

[8]

WALT WHITMAN AND HIS POEMS

"I celebrate myself,
And what I assume you shall assume,
For every atom belonging to me, as good as belongs
to you."

He leaves houses and their shuttered rooms,
for the open air. He drops disguise and ceremony, and walks forth with the confidence and
gayety of a child. For the old decorums of writing he substitutes new decorums. The first
glance out of his eyes electrifies him with love
and delight. He will have the earth receive and
return his affection; he will stay with it as the
bridegroom stays with the bride. The cool-
breath'd ground, the slumbering and liquid trees,
the just-gone sunset, the vitreous pour of the full
moon, the tender and growing night, he salutes
and touches, and they touch him. The sea supports him with its powerful and crooked fingers.
Dash me with amorous wet! then he says, I can
repay you.

By this writer the rules of polite circles are
dismissed with scorn. Your stale modesties, he
seems to say, are filthy to such a man as I.

[9]

RIVULETS OF PROSE

"I believe in the flesh and the appetites,
Seeing, hearing and feeling are miracles, and eacn
    part and tag of me is a miracle.
I do not press my finger across my mouth,
I keep as delicate around the bowels as around the
    head and heart,
Copulation is no more rank to me than death is."

No sniveller or skulker or tea-drinking poet or
puny person or prude is Walt Whitman. He will
bring poems fit to fill the days and nights—fit
for men and women with the attributes of throb-
bing blood and flesh. The body, he teaches, is
beautiful. Sex is also beautiful. Are you to be put
down, he seems to ask, to that shallow level of
literature and conversation that stops a man's
recognizing the delicious pleasure of his sex, or
a woman hers? Nature he proclaims inherently
clean. Sex will not be put aside; it is a great or-
dination of the universe. He works the muscle
of the male and the teeming fibre of the female
throughout his writings, as wholesome realities,
impure only by deliberate intention and effort.
To men and women he says, You can have
healthy and powerful breeds of children on no

less terms than these of mine. Follow me and
there shall be taller and richer crops of humanity
on the earth.

In the "Leaves of Grass" are the facts of eter-
nity and immortality largely treated. Happiness
is no dream and perfection is no dream. Amel-
ioration is my lesson, he says with calm voice, and
progress is my lesson and the lesson of all things.
Then his persuasion becomes a taunt, and his
love bitter and compulsory. With strong and
steady call he addresses men. Come, he seems
to say, from the midst of all that you have been
your whole life surrounding yourself with. Leave
all the preaching and teaching of others, and
mind only these words of mine.

"Long enough have you dreamed contemptible
    dreams,
Now I wash the gum from your eyes,
You must habit yourself to the dazzle of the light
    and of every moment of your life.

Long have you timidly waded, holding a plank by
    the shore,
Now I will you to be a bold swimmer,

[11]

RIVULETS OF PROSE

To jump off in the midst of the sea, and rise again
    and nod to me and shout, and laughingly dash
    with your hair.

I am the teacher of athletes,
He that by me spreads a wider breast than my own
    proves the width of my own,
He most honors my style who learns under it to
    destroy the teacher.

The boy I love, the same becomes a man not through
    derived power but in his own right,
Wicked, rather than virtuous out of conformity or
    fear,
Fond of his sweetheart, relishing well his steak,
Unrequited love or a slight cutting him worse than
    a wound cuts,
First rate to ride, to fight, to hit the bull's eye, to
    sail a skiff, to sing a song, or play on the banjo,
Preferring scars and faces pitted with smallpox over
    all latherers and those that keep out of the sun.

I teach straying from me, yet who can stray from me?
I follow you whoever you are from the present hour;
My words itch at your ears till you understand
    them.

WALT WHITMAN AND HIS POEMS

I do not say these things for a dollar, or to fill up
　　the time while I wait for a boat;
It is you talking just as much as myself. . . . I act
　　as the tongue of you,
It was tied in your mouth . . . in mine it begins
　　to be loosened.
I swear I will never mention love or death inside
　　a house,
And I swear I will never translate myself at all, only
　　to him or her who privately stays with me in
　　the open air."

The eleven other poems have each distinct
purposes, curiously veiled. Theirs is no writer to
be gone through with in a day or a month. Rather
it is his pleasure to elude you and provoke you
for deliberate purposes of his own.

Doubtless in the scheme this man has built
for himself the writing of poems is but a propor-
tionate part of the whole. It is plain that public
and private performance, politics, love, friendship, behaviour, the art of conversation, science,
society, the American people, the reception of the
great novelties of city and country, all have their
equal call upon him and receive equal attention.
In politics he could enter with the freedom and

[13]

reality he shows in poetry. His scope of life is the amplest of any yet in philosophy. He is the true spiritualist. He recognizes no annihilation or death or loss of identity. He is the largest lover and sympathizer that has appeared in literature. He loves the earth and sun and the animals. He does not separate the learned from the unlearned, the northerner from the southerner, the white from the black, or the native from the immigrant just landed at the wharf. Every one, he seems to say, appears excellent to me, every employment is adorned, and every male and female glorious.

"The press of my foot to the earth springs a hundred
    affections,
They scorn the best I can do to relate them.

I am enamored of growing outdoors,
Of men that live among cattle or taste of the ocean
    or woods,
Of the builders and steerers of ships, of the wielders
    of axes and mauls, of the drivers of horses,
I can eat and sleep with them week in and week
    out.

WALT WHITMAN AND HIS POEMS

What is commonest and cheapest and nearest and
    easiest is Me,
Me going in for my chances, spending for vast
    returns,
Adorning myself to bestow myself on the first that
    will take me,
Not asking the sky to come down to my goodwill,
Scattering it freely forever."

If health were not his distinguishing attribute
this poet would be the very harlot of persons.
Right and left he flings his arms, drawing men
and women with undeniable love to his close em-
brace, loving the clasp of their hands, the touch
of their necks and breasts, and the sound of their
voices. All seems to burn up under his fierce affection for persons. Politics, religions, institutions, art, quickly fall aside before them. In the
whole universe, he says, I see nothing more divine
than human souls.

"When the psalm sings instead of singer,
When the script preaches instead of the preacher,
When the pulpit descends and goes instead of the
    carver that carved the supporting desk,
When the sacred vessels of the bits of the eucharist, or

[15]

RIVULETS OF PROSE

the lath and plast procreate as effectually as the
young silversmiths or bakers, or the masons in
their overalls,
When a university course convinces like a slumbering
woman and child convince,
When the minted gold in the vault smiles like the
nightwatchman's daughter,
When warantee deeds loaf in chairs opposite and are
my friendly companions,
I intend to reach them my hand and make as much
of them as I make of men and women."

Who then is that insolent unknown? Who is
it, praising himself as if others were not fit to do
it, and coming rough and unbidden among
writers to unsettle what was settled, and to rev-
olutionize in fact our modern civilization? Walt
Whitman was born on Long Island, on the hills
about thirty miles from the greatest American
city, on the last day of May, 1819, and has grown
up in Brooklyn and New York to be thirty-six
years old, to enjoy perfect health, and to understand his country and its spirit.

Interrogations more than this, and that will
not be put off unanswered, spring continually

[16]

WALT WHITMAN AND HIS POEMS

through the perusal of these "Leaves of Grass:"

If there were to be selected, out of the incalculable volumes of printed matter in existence, any single work to stand for America and her times, should this be the work?

Must not the true American poet absorb all others, and present a new and far more ample and vigorous type?

Has not the time arrived for a school of live writing and tuition consistent with the principles of these poems? consistent with the free spirit of this age, and with the American truths of politics? consistent with geology, and astronomy, and phrenology, and human physiology? consistent with the sublimity of immortality and the directness of common sense?

If in this poem the United States have found their poetic voice and taken measure and form, is it any more than a beginning? Walt Whitman himself disclaims singularity in his work, and announces the coming after him of great successions of poets, and that he but lifts his finger to give the signal.

Was he not needed? Has not literature been bred in and in long enough? Has it not become unbearably artificial?

Shall a man of faith and practice in the simplicity of real things be called eccentric, while the disciple of the fictitious school writes without question?

Shall it still be the amazement of the light and dark that freshness of expression is the rarest quality of all?

You have come in good time, Walt Whitman! In opinions, in manners, in costumes, in books, in the aims and occupancy of life, in associates, in poems, conformity to all unnatural and tainted customs passes without remark; while perfect naturalness, health, faith, self-reliance, and all primal expressions of the manliest love and friendship, subject one to the stare and controversy of the world.

BOZ AND DEMOCRACY

From the February 26th, 1842, issue of "Brother Jonathan."

Is it not your fortune, reader, occasionally, in your path through life, to meet with one whose custom it is to look always upon the dark points of a picture—to seek out faults, and where they do not really exist, to fancy them—whose disposition is sour and whose soul seems anxious to condemn all that other people praise? A man of this description is to cheerfulness and soul-confidence what a cloud is to the sun. Malignant and envious, he would rob a patriot of his countrymen's love—a saint of his reverence a glorious writer of his well-deserved fame.

The Washington Globe discourseth after the following manner:

"If to delineate the human character in its lowest stage of ignorance, vice and degradation, and give it the most unbounded scope in every species of wicked-

[19]

ness and crime, is to be a Democratic writer, then most assuredly Mr. Dickens is emphatically one. He has exhibited human nature in its naked, ragged deformity, reeking with vice and pollution; as ignorant as wicked, and absolutely below the standard of the very beasts of the field. He has made his exhibitions of human character more disgusting and abhorrent, by a degree of brutal ignorance and stupendous depravity, which constitute, in their combination, a spectacle so absolutely and exclusively hateful, as to absorb all consideration of the means by which this miserable desecration of humanity was produced, and all sympathy for the brutes who to us, as it were, misrepresent their fellow creatures. Incidentally, these spectacles may connect themselves in our minds, with the means by which this extremity of vice and ignorance was produced, but the overwhelming feeling is that of disgust and abhorrence. There are physical diseases, so revolting to the senses, as to convert pity into sickening disgust, and there is a degree of moral corruption and wickedness which annihilates all sympathy.

"To call this the literature of Democracy is to make Democracy as brutal as this gentleman has been pleased to represent it in his native country. It may suit there, where it has perhaps its prototypes, so numerous as to constitute a class, but it does not actually belong to the United States, nor is it applicable to the state of society in this country. Such a school of literature can only aid the course and progress of vice among us, by placing before the already degraded, examples of new modes of wickedness, with which they were hitherto unacquainted, and degrees of degradation of which they never had any perception, until they became so conspicuous in the polite and fashionable literature of the day. The extraordinary cheapness with which these works have been got up among us, and the allurements they present in a series of embellishments corresponding with the grossness of the scenes they are intended to illustrate, have given them a general circulation among those classes most likely to overlook the latent imperceptible moral, if any such exists, and to concentrate their attention on those broad caricatures of wickedness, which are too often represented by the author in combination with ludicrous circumstances, admirably calculated to make those who have no very distinct notions of right and wrong, consider the whole an excellent joke, worthy of all imitation.

"I cannot, for my part, comprehend how a writer can be fairly entitled to the credit of being the champion of that class of mankind which he pictures in colors so revolting to our feelings and sympathies; nor by what process of induction this intimate association with this perpetual contemplation of all the varieties of extreme degradation, coupled with a boundless latitude of crime, can be converted into a school of morals. If this is indeed the tendency of such contemplations and associations, let us send our children to bridewells and penitentiaries for their education, and to the quarter sessions for lessons of morality. Indeed it seems to me that Mr. Dickens's moral writings are very much on a par with Le Bœuf's great moral picture of Adam and Eve, in the moment of being tempted by the serpent. They were represented as large as life, perfectly naked, the female in the attitude of a lascivious courtesan, tempting a bashful youth; and if the artist had not fortunately bethought himself of calling it a great moral picture, no decent female would have dared to visit its exhibition. At this rate, I should not be at all surprised at seeing some strenuous amateur writing a criticism to prove the displays of Fanny Elssler a great moral spectacle."

The above is evidently the offering of no unpracticed hand. I wish I could speak as favorably of the author's appreciation of merit, and of his candor and judgment.

A "democratic writer," I take it, is one, the tendency of whose pages is, to destroy those old landmarks which pride and fashion have set up, making impassable distinctions between the brethren of the Great Family—to render in their deformity before us the tyranny of partial laws —to show us the practical workings of the thousand distortions engrafted by custom upon our notions of what justice is—to make us love our fellow-creatures, and own that although social distinctions place others far higher or far lower than we, yet are human beings alike, as links of the same chain; one whose lines are imbued, from preface to finis, with that philosophy which teaches to pull down the high and bring up the low. I consider Mr. Dickens to be a democratic writer.

The mere fact of a man's delineating human character in its lowest stages of degradation, and giving it unbounded scope in every species of wickedness, proves neither his "democracy" nor its opposite. If it be done in such a way, as that a kind of charm is thrown all the time around the guilty personage described—in such a way that excuses and palliations for his vice are covertly conveyed, every now and then—such writings most assuredly, would have no fair claim to rank among "the literature of democracy." But

[23]

when these specimens of naked, ragged deformity, as ignorant as wicked, are drawn out before
us, and surrounded with their fit accompaniments, filth and darkness, and the deepest dis-
comfort—when crime is portrayed, never so that
by any possibility the reader can find the slightest temptation to go and do likewise—when we
see how evil doing is followed by its sure and
long and weary punishment—when our minds
are led to the irresistible conclusion that in-
iquity is loathsome, and by the magic of the pen-
painter, have his pictures so stamped upon them
that we ever after associate depraved actions
with lowness and the very vulgarity of pollution
—in such case, I say, the delineations of life in
its lowest aspect, and even characterized by
grossest ignorance and brutality, do not militate
against their author's claim for admiration from
all true democrats. And, then, the effect of the
contrast which Mr. Dickens seems fond of forc-
ing us to make between these wicked ones, and
the beings of purity and truth whom he also
draws with a master hand! How he brings these
characters together, and places them side by side,

and makes them play into each other's hands, as it were, for the purpose of bringing out their distinctive traits! He not only teaches his readers to abhor vice, but he exhibits before them, for imitation, examples of the beauty of honesty—not as in the abstract style of the essayist, or the lofty dreams of the poet—but by examples that everyone can copy, examples in familiar life, that come home to us all. Who is not in love with truth when he follows, through trouble, poverty, and temptation, a little child that never swerves, but in its simplicity conducts as though there were no such thing as falsehood? What impropriety is there in the process of induction which calls that a school of morals—where the pupil sees mapped out before him the parish boy's progress through sin and ignorance—resisting the tempter when yielding would have procured ease —steadily holding to the truth at all risks—living like an angel of light amid the spirit of darkness—never giving up, though often his prospect seemed desperate—and being rewarded, at last, with prosperity?

The writer in the Globe thinks that the spec-

[25]

tacles of misery pictured in the Boz novels constitute a combination so exclusively hateful, as
to absorb all consideration of the means which
produce them, and all sympathy for the per-
formers themselves. Did not the writer in the
Globe, when he read the graphically drawn and
deeply colored picture of the life led by Oliver
Twist and his mates in the poorhouse, and of
all the transactions there—and of the conduct
of those who had to do with the institution—did
he not have some reflections upon the evils of
such a state of society as led to the existence of
these things? When he read of Squeers and Do-
theboys Hall did he not entertain the most distant idea of how such a boarding-school system,
if prevalent, might be rooted out by thus showing it up?

The critic in the Globe compares Mr. Dickens's portraitures to the exhibition of those physical diseases so revolting to the senses as to create
nothing but horror and sickening disgust. I suppose that in order to please our critic, a writer
must speak mincingly, and with much delicacy
lest he should introduce a vigorous turn or idea,

which would offend him for its grossness. I fear me he is too dainty. Such exquisite sensitiveness—such affectation of being overcome by the strength of description in the novelist—such refined horror at some fancied overstepping of the limits wherein an author should confine himself, if he aspires to please the polite taste—bespeak the literary fop, much more than they mark a man really fit to measure the length and breadth of that genius he so maligns. Besides, Mr. Dickens makes a sparing use of these strong features. The criticism in the Globe seems imbued throughout with the notion that the Boz works tell of nothing but the horrible and the awful—of desperate crime, and sensual vice. Surely it is not so. Boz is not altogether a feeder upon Newgate Calendars, and Police Reports, and whatever else reflects from the mind of him who looks thereon a sombre and a sorrowful hue. Pickwick, and the Wellers, and the Fat Boy, forbid! Dick Swiveller and the Marchioness—Kit, and pony—Miggs and Joe Willett, condemn the imputation! And thy sweet face, Kate Nickleby, —and thy Christian nature, Cheeryble Brothers

[27]

—and thou, poor Nell—and thou, G. Varden—
repel the slander!

The familiarity with low life wherein Mr.
Dickens places his readers, is a wholesome familiarity. For those moving in a kindred sphere it
is wholesome, because it holds out to them continually the spectacle of beings of their own
grade, engaged either in worthy actions which
are held up to emulation, and shown to be rewarded both in themselves and in their results—
or engaged in avocations of guilt which in themselves and their results are fearful, and only to
be thought of with shuddering. For the richer
classes this familiarity is wholesome because they
are taught to feel, in fancy, what poverty is,
and what thousands of fellow-creatures, as good
as they, toil year after year, amid discourage-
ments and evils, whose bare relation is enough
to make the hearer heart-sick. The rich cannot
taste the distresses of want from their own experience; it is something if they are made to do
so through the power of the pen.

He cannot comprehend, this critic tells us,
how a writer can be called the champion of that

class of mankind which he pictures in colors so revolting. A good parent or teacher sometimes has to lay before those whom he would reform, the strong, naked, hideous truth. But Mr. Dickens never maligns the poor. He puts the searing iron to wickedness, whether among poor or rich; and yet when he describes the guilty, poor and oppressed man, we are always in some way reminded how much need there is that certain systems of law and habit which lead to this poverty and consequent crime should be remedied.

I would say more, but my limits prevent me. I cannot, however, close this paper, without alluding once more, as in the beginning of the article, to those men who are always prone to carping and detraction. Mr. Dickens's charming manners, his modesty, his freedom from haughtiness, his *lovable* nature, his pleasant tenor of mind, as displayed in his personal conduct— might, it would seem, have saved him from those snappish and sour flings which some of the third-rate editorial fry are indulging in toward him. There are men among us with that unfortunate disposition—unfortunate as well for themselves as for those who have any intercourse with them —which picks out by preference every chance to snarl, bite, and find fault. Honor paid to a fellow-creature is hateful to them: they turn pale with envy and malignance.

As I think that my humble lance, wielded in defense of Mr. Dickens, may meet the sight of that gentleman himself, I cannot lose the opportunity of saying how much I love and esteem him for what he has taught me through his writings —and for the genial influence that these writings spread around them wherever they go. Never having seen Boz in the body, we have yet had many a tête-à-tête. And I cannot tamely hear one whom I have long considered as a personal friend, and as a friend to his species, thus falsely and uncharitably, and groundlessly attacked.

MY TRIBUTE TO FOUR POETS

From Specimen Days & Collect (*Philadelphia,* 1882–3).

A SHORT but pleasant visit to Longfellow. I am not one of the calling kind, but as the author of "Evangeline" kindly took the trouble to come to see me three years ago in Camden, where I was ill, I felt not only the impulse of my own pleasure on that occasion, but a duty. He was the only particular eminence I called on in Boston, and I shall not soon forget his lit-up face and the glowing warmth and courtesy, in the modes of what is called the old school.

And now just here I feel the impulse to interpolate something about the mighty four who stamp this first American century with its birthmarks of poetic literature. In a late magazine one of my reviewers, who ought to know better, speaks of my "attitude of contempt and scorn and intolerance" toward the leading poets—of

[31]

my "deriding" them, and preaching their "use-
lessness." If anybody cares to know what I think
—and have long thought and avow'd—about
them, I am entirely willing to propound. I can't
imagine any better luck befalling these States for
a poetical beginning and initiation than has come
from Emerson, Longfellow, Bryant, and Whittier. Emerson, to me, stands unmistakably at the
head, but for the others I am at a loss where to
give any precedence. Each illustrious, each
rounded, each distinctive. Emerson for his sweet,
vital-tasting melody, rhym'd philosophy, and
poems as amber-clear as the honey of the wild bee
he loves to sing. Longfellow for rich color, grace-
ful forms and incidents—all that makes life
beautiful and love refined—competing with the
singers of Europe on their own ground, and, with
one exception, better and finer work than that of
any of them. Bryant pulsing the first interior
verse-throbs of a mighty world—bard of the
river and the wood, ever conveying a taste of
open air, with scents as from hayfields, grapes,
and birch-border—always lurkingly fond of
threnodies—beginning and ending his long career

with chants of death, with here and there through all, poems, or passages of poems, touching the highest universal truths, enthusiasms, duties—morals as grim and eternal, if not as stormy and fateful, as anything in Eschylus. While in Whittier, with his special themes—(his outcropping love of heroism and war, for all his Quakerdom, his verses at times like the measur'd step of Cromwell's old veterans)—in Whittier lives the zeal, the moral energy, that founded New England—the splendid rectitude and ardor of Luther, Milton, George Fox—I must not, dare not, say the wilfulness and narrowness—though doubtless the world needs now, and always will need, almost above all, just such narrowness and wilfulness.

BRITISH LITERATURE

From Specimen Days & Collect (Philadelphia, 1882-3).

To avoid mistake, I would say that I not only commend the study of this literature, but wish our sources of supply and comparison vastly enlarged. American students may well derive from all former lands—from forenoon Greece and Rome, down to the perturb'd medieval times, the Crusades, and so to Italy, the German intellect—all the older literatures and all the newer ones—from witty and warlike France, and markedly, and in many ways, and at many different periods, from the enterprise and soul of the great Spanish race—bearing ourselves always courteous, always deferential, indebted beyond measure to the mother-world, to all its nations dead, as all its nations living—the offspring, this America of ours, the daughter, not by any means of the British Isles exclusively, but of the continent, and all continents. Indeed, it is time we should realize and fully fructify those germs we also hold from Italy, France, Spain, especially in the best imaginative productions of those lands, which are, in many ways, loftier and subtler than the English, or British, and indispensable to complete our service, proportions, education, reminiscences, &c. . . . The British element these States hold, and have always held, enormously beyond its fit proportions. I have already spoken of Shakspere. He seems to me of astral genius, first class, entirely fit for feudalism. His contributions, especially to the literature of the passions, are immense, forever dear to humanity—and his name is always to be reverenced in America. But there is much in him ever offensive to democracy. He is not only the tally of feudalism, but I should say Shakspere is incarnated, uncompromising feudalism, in literature. Then one seems to detect something in him—I hardly know how to describe it—even amid the dazzle of his genius; and, in inferior manifestations, it is found in nearly all leading British authors. (Perhaps we will have to import the words Snob, Snobbish,

[35]

&c., after all.) While of the great poems of Asian antiquity, the Indian epics, the book of Job, the Ionian Iliad, the unsurpassedly simple, loving, perfect idyls of the life and death of Christ, in the New Testament, (indeed Homer and the Biblical utterances intertwine familiarly with us, in the main,) and along down, of most of the characteristic, imaginative or romantic relics of the continent, as the Cid, Cervantes's Don Quixote, &c., I should say they substantially adjust themselves to us, and, far off as they are, accord curiously with our bed and board to-day, in New York, Washington, Canada, Ohio, Texas, California—and with our notions, both of seriousness and of fun, and our standards of heroism, manliness, and even the democratic requirements—those requirements are not only not fulfilled in the Shakesperean productions, but are insulted on every page.

I add that—while England is among the greatest of lands in political freedom, or the idea of it, and in stalwart personal character, &c.— the spirit of English literature is not great, at least is not greatest—and its products are no models for us. With the exception of Shakspere, there is no first-class genius in that literature—which, with a truly vast amount of value, and of artificial beauty, (largely from the classics,) is almost always material, sensual, not spiritual—almost always congests, makes plethoric, not frees, expands, dilates—is cold, anti-democratic, loves to be sluggish and stately, and shows much of that characteristic of vulgar persons, the dread of saying or doing something not at all improper in itself, but unconventional, and that may be laugh'd at. In its best, the sombre pervades it; it is moody, melancholy, and, to give it its due, expresses, in characters and plots, those qualities, in an unrival'd manner. Yet not as the black thunder-storms, and in great normal, crashing passions, of the Greek dramatists—clearing the air, refreshing afterward, bracing with power; but as in Hamlet, moping, sick, uncertain, and leaving ever after a secret taste for the blues, the morbid fascination, the luxury of wo. . . .

I strongly recommend all the young men and young women of the United States to whom it may be eligible, to overhaul the well-freighted fleets, the literatures of Italy, Spain, France, Germany, so full of those elements of freedom, self-possession, gay-heartedness, subtlety, dilation, needed in preparations for the future of the States. I only wish we could have really good translations. I rejoice at the feeling for Oriental researches and poetry, and hope it will go on.

EDGAR POE'S SIGNIFICANCE

From Specimen Days & Collect (Philadelphia, 1882–3).

In diagnosing this disease called humanity—to assume for the nonce what seems a chief mood of the personality and writings of my subject—I have thought that poets, somewhere or other on the list, present the most mark'd indications. Comprehending artists in a mass, musicians, painters, actors, and so on, and considering each and all of them as radiations or flanges of that furious-whirling wheel, poetry, the centre and axis of the whole, where else indeed may we so well investigate the causes, growths, tally-marks of the time—the age's matter and malady?

By common consent there is nothing better for man or woman than a perfect and noble life, morally without flaw, happily balanced in activity, physically sound and pure, giving its due proportion, and no more, to the sympathetic, the

[39]

human emotional element—a life, in all these, unhasting, unresting, untiring to the end. And yet there is another shape of personality dearer far to the artist-sense, (which likes the play of strongest lights and shades,) where the perfect character, the good, the heroic, although never attain'd, is never lost sight of, but through failures, sorrows, temporary downfalls, is return'd to again and again, and while often violated, is passionately adhered to as long as mind, muscles, voice, obey the power we call volition. This sort of personality we see more or less in Burns, Byron, Schiller, and George Sand. But we do not see it in Edgar Poe. (All this is the result of reading at intervals the last three days a new volume of his poems—I took it on my rambles down by the pond, and by degrees read it all through there.) While to the character first outlined the service Poe renders is certainly that entire contrast and contradiction which is next best to fully exemplifying it.

Almost without the first sign of moral principle, or of the concrete or its heroisms, or the simpler affections of the heart, Poe's verses illustrate an intense faculty for technical and abstract beauty, with the rhyming art to excess, an incorrigible propensity toward nocturnal themes, a demoniac undertone behind every page —and, by final judgment, probably belong among the electric lights of imaginative literature, brilliant and dazzling, but with no heat. There is an indescribable magnetism about the poet's life and reminiscences, as well as the poems. To one who could work out their subtle retracing and retrospect, the latter would make a close tally no doubt between the author's birth and antecedents, his childhood and youth, his physique, his so-call'd education, his studies and associates, the literary and social Baltimore, Richmond, Philadelphia and New York, of those times—not only the places and circumstances in themselves, but often, very often, in a strange spurning of and reaction from them all.

The following from a report in the Washington "Star" of November 16, 1875, may afford those who care for it something further of my point of view toward this interesting figure and influence of our era. There occurr'd about that date in Baltimore a public reburial of Poe's remains, and dedication of a monument over the grave:

"Being in Washington on a visit at the time, 'the old gray' went over to Baltimore, and though ill from paralysis, consented to hobble up and silently take a seat on the platform, but refused to make any speech, saying, 'I have felt strong impulse to come over and be here to-day myself in memory of Poe, which I have obey'd, but not the slightest impulse to make a speech, which, my dear friends, must also be obeyed.' In an informal circle, however, in conversation after the ceremonies, Whitman said: 'For a long while, and until lately, I had a distaste for Poe's writings. I wanted, and still want for poetry, the clear sun shining, and fresh air blowing—the strength and power of health, not of delirium, even amid the stormiest passions—with always the background of the eternal moralities. Non-complying with these requirements, Poe's genius has yet conquer'd a special recognition for itself, and I too have come to fully admit it, and appreciate it and him.

" 'In a dream I once had, I saw a vessel on the sea, at midnight, in a storm. It was no great full-rigg'd ship, nor majestic steamer steering firmly through the gale, but seem'd one of those su-

[42]

perb little schooner yachts I had often seen lying anchor'd, rocking so jauntily, in the waters around New York, or up Long Island Sound—now flying uncontroll'd with torn sails and broken spars through the wild sleet and winds and waves of the night. On the deck was a slender, slight, beautiful figure, a dim man, apparently enjoying all the terror, the murk, and the dislocation of which he was the centre and the victim. That figure of my lurid dream might stand for Edgar Poe, his spirit, his fortunes, and his poems—themselves all lurid dreams.' "

Much more may be said, but I most desired to exploit the idea put at the beginning. By its popular poets the calibres of an age, the weak spots of its embankments, its sub-currents, (often more significant than the biggest surface ones,) are unerringly indicated. The lush and the weird that have taken such extraordinary possession of Nineteenth Century verse-lovers—what mean they? The inevitable tendency of poetic culture to morbidity, abnormal beauty—the sickliness of all technical thought or refinement in itself—the abnegation of the perennial and democratic concretes at first hand, the body, the earth and sea,

[43]

sex and the like—and the substitution of something for them at second or third hand—what
bearings have they on current pathological
study?

THE BIBLE AS POETRY

From November Boughs (Philadelphia, 1888).

I SUPPOSE one cannot at this day say anything
new, from a literary point of view, about those
autochthonic bequests of Asia—the Hebrew
Bible, the mighty Hindu epics, and a hundred
lesser but typical works; (not now definitely
including the Iliad—though that work was certainly of Asiatic genesis, as Homer himself was—
considerations which seem curiously ignored).
But will there ever be a time or place—ever a
student, however modern, of the grand art, to
whom those compositions will not afford pro-
founder lessons than all else of their kind in the
garnerage of the past? Could there be any more
opportune suggestion, to the current popular
writer and reader of verse, what the office of poet
was in primeval times—and is yet capable of
being, anew, adjusted entirely to the modern?

[45]

RIVULETS OF PROSE

All the poems of Orientalism, with the Old and New Testaments at the centre, tend to deep and wide, (I don't know but the deepest and widest,) psychological development—with little, or nothing at all, of the mere æsthetic, the principal verse-requirement of our day. Very late, but unerringly, comes to every capable student the perception that it is not in beauty, it is not in art, it is not even in science, that the profoundest laws of the case have their eternal sway and outcropping.

In his discourse on "Hebrew Poets" De Sola Mendes said: "The fundamental feature of Judaism, of the Hebrew nationality, was religion; its poetry was naturally religious. Its subjects, God and Providence, the covenants with Israel, God in Nature, and as reveal'd, God the Creator and Governor, Nature in her majesty and beauty, inspired hymns and odes to Nature's God. And then the checker'd history of the nation furnish'd allusions, illustrations, and subjects for epic display—the glory of the sanctuary, the offerings, the splendid ritual, the Holy City, and lov'd Palestine with its pleasant valleys and wild

[46]

tracts." Dr. Mendes said "that rhyming was not
a characteristic of Hebrew poetry at all. Metre
was not a necessary mark of poetry. Great poets
discarded it; the early Jewish poets knew it not."

Compared with the famed epics of Greece, and
lesser ones since, the spinal supports of the Bible
are simple and meager. All its history, biography,
narratives, etc., are as beads, strung on and indi-
cating the eternal thread of the Deific purpose
and power. Yet with only deepest faith for impetus, and such Deific purpose for palpable or
impalpable theme, it often transcends the masterpieces of Hellas, and all masterpieces. The meta-
phors daring beyond account, the lawless soul,
extravagant by our standards, the glow of love
and friendship, the fervent kiss—nothing in argument or logic, but unsurpass'd in proverbs, in
religious ecstacy, in suggestions of common mor-
tality and death, man's great equalizers—the
spirit everything, the ceremonies and forms of
the churches nothing, faith limitless, its immense
sensuousness immensely spiritual—an incredible,
all-inclusive non-worldliness and dew-scented il-
literacy (the antipodes of our Nineteenth

Century business absorption and morbid refinement)—no hair-splitting doubts, no sickly sulk-
ing and sniffling, no "Hamlet," no "Adonais,"
no "Thanatopsis," no "In Memoriam."

The culminated proof of the poetry of a
country is the quality of its personnel, which, in
any race, can never be really superior without
superior poems. The finest blending of individuality with universality (in my opinion nothing
out of the galaxies of the "Iliad," or Shakspere's
heroes, or from the Tennysonian "Idyls," so
lofty, devoted and starlike,) typified in the songs
of those old Asiatic lands. Men and women as
great columnar trees. Nowhere else the abnegation of self towering in such quaint sublimity;
nowhere else the simplest human emotions con-
quering the gods of heaven, and fate itself. (The
episode, for instance, toward the close of the
"Mahabharata"—the journey of the wife Savitri
with the god of death, Yama,

"One terrible to see—blood-red his garb,
His body huge and dark, bloodshot his eyes,
Which flamed like suns beneath his turban cloth,
Arm'd was he with a noose,"

[48]

who carries off the soul of the dead husband, the wife tenaciously following, and—by the resistless charm of perfect poetic recitation!—eventually redeeming her captive mate.)

I remember how enthusiastically William H. Seward, in his last days, once expatiated on these themes, from his travels in Turkey, Egypt, and Asia Minor, finding the oldest Biblical narratives exactly illustrated there to-day with apparently no break or change along three thousand years— the veil'd women, the costumes, the gravity and simplicity, all the manners just the same. The veteran Trelawney said he found the only real *nobleman* of the world in a good average specimen of the mid-aged or elderly Oriental. In the East the grand figure, always leading, is the *old man*, majestic, with flowing beard, paternal, etc. In Europe and America, it is, as we know, the young fellow—in novels, a handsome and interesting hero, more or less juvenile—in operas, a tenor with blooming cheeks, black mustache, superficial animation, and perhaps good lungs, but no more depth than skim-milk. But reading folks probably get their information of those

[49]

Bible areas and current peoples, as depicted in print by English and French cads, the most shallow, impudent, supercilious brood on earth.

I have said nothing yet of the cumulus of associations (perfectly legitimate parts of its influence, and finally in many respects the dominant parts,) of the Bible as a poetic entity, and of every portion of it. Not the old edifice only— the congeries also of events and struggles and surroundings, of which it has been the scene and motive—even the horrors, dreads, deaths. How many ages and generations have brooded and wept and agonized over this book! What untellable joys and ecstasies—what support to martyrs at the stake—from it. (No really great song can ever attain full purport till long after the death of its singer—till it has accrued and incorporated the many passions, many joys and sorrows, it has itself arous'd.) To what myriads has it been the shore and rock of safety—the refuge from driving tempest and wreck! Translated in all languages, how it has united this diverse world! Of civilized lands to-day, whose of our retrospects has it not interwoven and link'd and permeated? Not only does it bring us what is clasp'd within its covers; nay, that is the least of what it brings. Of its thousands, there is not a verse, not a word, but is thick-studded with human emotions, successions of fathers and sons, mothers and daughters, of our own antecedents, inseparable from that background of us, on which, phantasmal as it is, all that we are to-day inevitably depends—our ancestry, our past.

Strange, but true, that the principal factor in cohering the nations, eras and paradoxes of the globe, by giving them a common platform of two or three great ideas, a commonalty of origin, and projecting cosmic brotherhood, the dream of all hope, all time—that the long trains, gestations, attempts and failures, resulting in the New World, and in modern solidarity and politics— are to be identified and resolv'd back into a collection of old poetic lore, which, more than any one thing else, has been the axis of civilization and history through thousands of years—and except for which this America of ours, with its polity and essentials, could not now be existing.

No true bard will ever contravene the Bible.

RIVULETS OF PROSE

If the time ever comes when iconoclasm does its extremest in one direction against the Books of the Bible in its present form, the collection must still survive in another, and dominate just as much as hitherto, or more than hitherto, through its divine and primal poetic structure. To me, that is the living and definite element-principle of the work, evolving everything else. Then the continuity; the oldest and newest Asiatic utterance and character, and all between, holding together, like the apparition of the sky, and coming to us the same. Even to our Nineteenth Century here are the fountain heads of song.

OUR EMINENT VISITORS

PAST, PRESENT AND FUTURE

From November Boughs (Philadelphia, 1888).

WELCOME to them each and all! They do good
—the deepest, widest, most needed good—though
quite certainly not in the ways attempted—
which have, at times, something irresistibly
comic. What can be more farcical, for instance,
than the sight of a worthy gentleman coming
three or four thousand miles through wet and
wind to speak complacently and at great length
on matters of which he both entirely mistakes or
knows nothing—before crowds of auditors
equally complacent, and equally at fault?

Yet welcome and thanks, we say, to those
visitors we have, and have had, from abroad
among us—and may the procession continue!
We have had Dickens and Thackeray, Froude,

[53]

RIVULETS OF PROSE

Herbert Spencer, Oscar Wilde, Lord Coleridge—soldiers, savants, poets—and now Matthew Arnold and Irving the actor. Some have come to make money—some for a "good time"—some to help us along and give us advice—and some undoubtedly to investigate, *bona fide*, this great problem, democratic America, looming upon the world with such cumulative power through a hundred years, now with the evident intention (since the Secession War) to stay, and take a leading hand, for many a century to come, in civilization's and humanity's eternal game. But alas! that very investigation—the method of that investigation—is where the deficit most surely and helplessly comes in. Let not Lord Coleridge and Mr. Arnold (to say nothing of the illustrious actor) imagine that when they have met and survey'd the etiquettical gatherings of our wealthy, distinguish'd and sure-to-be-put-forward-on-such-occasions citizens (New York, Boston, Philadelphia, &c., have certain stereotyped strings of them, continually lined and paraded like the lists of dishes at hotel tables—you are sure to get the same over and over again

[54]

OUR EMINENT VISITORS

—it is very amusing)—and the bowing and in-
troducing, the receptions at the swell clubs, the
eating and drinking and praising and praising
back—and the next day riding about Central
Park, or doing the "Public Institutions"—and so
passing through, one after another, the full-dress
coteries of the Atlantic cities, all grammatical
and cultured and correct, with the toned-down
manners of the gentlemen, and the kid-gloves,
and luncheon and finger-glasses—Let not our
eminent visitors, we say, suppose that, by means
of these experiences, they have "seen America,"
or captur'd any distinctive clew or purport
thereof. Not a bit of it. Of the pulse-beats that
lie within and vitalize this Commonweal to-day
—of the hard-pan purports and idiosyncrasies
pursued faithfully and triumphantly by its bulk
of men North and South, generation after
generation, superficially unconscious of their
own aims, yet none the less pressing onward with
deathless intuition—those coteries do not furnish the faintest scintilla. In the Old World the
best flavor and significance of a race may possibly
need to be look'd for in its "upper classes," its

gentries, its courts, its *état major*. In the United States the rule is revers'd. Besides (and a point, this, perhaps, deepest of all,) the special marks of our grouping and design are not going to be understood in a hurry. The lesson and scanning right on the ground are difficult; I was going to say they are impossible to foreigners—but I have occasionally found the clearest appreciation of all coming from far-off quarters. Surely nothing could be more apt, not only for our eminent visitors present and to come, but for home study, than the following editorial criticism of the London *Times* on Mr. Froude's visit and lectures here a few years ago, and the culminating dinner given at Delmonico's, with its brilliant array of guests:

"We read the list," (says the *Times*), "of those who assembled to do honor to Mr. Froude: there were Mr. Emerson, Mr. Beecher, Mr. Curtis, Mr. Bryant; we add the names of those who sent letters of regret that they could not attend in person—Mr. Longfellow, Mr. Whittier. They are names which are well known—almost as well known and as much honor'd in England as in America; and yet what must we say in the end? The American people outside this assemblage of writers is something vaster and greater than they, singly or together, can comprehend. It cannot be said of any or of all of them that they can speak for their nation. We who look on at this distance are able perhaps on that account to see the more clearly that there are qualities of the American people which find no representation, no voice, among these their spokesmen. And what is true of them is true of the English class of whom Mr. Froude may be said to be the ambassador. Mr. Froude is master of a charming style. He has the gift of grace and the gift of sympathy. Taking any single character as the subject of his study, he may succeed after a very short time in so comprehending its workings as to be able to present a living figure to the intelligence and memory of his readers. But the movements of a nation, *the voiceless purpose of a people which cannot put its own thoughts into words, yet acts upon them in each successive generation*—these things do not lie within his grasp. . . . The functions of literature such as he represents are limited in their action; the influence he can wield is artificial and restricted, and, while he and his hearers please and are pleas'd with pleasant periods, his great mass of national life will flow around them unmov'd in its tides by action as powerless as that of the dwellers by the shore to direct the currents of the ocean."

[57]

RIVULETS OF PROSE

A thought, here, needs to be echoed, expanded, permanently treasured by our literary classes and educators. (The gestation, the youth, the knitting preparations, are now over, and it is full time for definite purpose, result.) How few think of it, though it is the impetus and background of our whole Nationality and popular life. In the present brief memorandum I very likely for the first time awake "the intelligent reader" to the idea and inquiry whether there isn't such a thing as the distinctive genius of our democratic New World, universal, immanent, bringing to a head the best experience of the past—not specially literary or intellectual —not merely "good," (in the Sunday School and Temperance Society sense,)—some invisible spine and great sympathetic to these States, resident only in the average people, in their practical life, in their physiology, in their emotions, in their nebulous yet fiery patriotism, in the armies (both sides) through the whole Secession War—an identity and character which indeed so far "finds no voice among their spokesmen."

To my mind America, vast and fruitful as it

appears to-day, is even yet, for its most important results, entirely in the tentative state; its very formation-stir and whirling trials and essays more splendid and picturesque, to my thinking, than the accomplish'd growths and shows of other lands, through European history, or Greece, or all the past. Surely a New World literature, worthy the name, is not to be, if it ever comes, some fiction, or fancy, or bit of sentimentalism or polish'd work merely by itself, or in abstraction. So long as such literature is no born branch and offshoot of the Nationality, rooted and grown from its roots, and fibred with its fibre, it can never answer any deep call or perennial need. Perhaps the untaught Republic is wiser than its teachers. The best literature is always a result of something far greater than itself—not the hero, but the portrait of the hero. Before there can be recorded history or poem there must be the transaction. Beyond the old masterpieces, the Iliad, the interminable Hindu epics, the Greek tragedies, even the Bible itself, range the immense facts of what must have preceded them, their *sine qua non*—the veritable poems and masterpieces, of which, grand as they are, the word-statements are but shreds and cartoons.

For to-day and the States, I think the vividest, rapidest, most stupendous processes ever known, ever perform'd by man or nation, on the largest scales and in countless varieties, are now and here presented. Not as our poets and preachers are always conventionally putting it—but quite different. Some colossal foundry, the flaming of the fire, the melted metal, the pounding trip-hammer, the surging crowds of workmen shifting from point to point, the murky shadows, the rolling haze, the discord, the crudeness, the deafening din, the disorder, the dross and clouds of dust, the waste and extravagance of material, the shafts of darted sunshine through the vast open roof-scuttles aloft—the mighty castings, many of them not yet fitted, perhaps delay'd long, yet each in its due time, with definite place and use and meaning—Such, more like, is a symbol of America.

After all of which, returning to our starting-point, reiterate, and in the whole Land's name, a welcome to our eminent guests. Visits like theirs, and hospitalities, and hand-shaking, and face meeting face, and the distant brought near —what divine solvents they are! Travel, reciprocity, "interviewing," intercommunion of lands—what are they but Democracy's and the highest Law's best aids? O that our own country —that every land in the world—could annually, continually, receive the poets, thinkers, scientists, even the official magnates, of other lands, as honor'd guests. O that the United States, especially the West, could have had a good long visit and explorative jaunt, from the noble and melancholy Tourguéneff, before he died—or from Victor Hugo—or Thomas Carlyle. Castelar, Tennyson, any of the two or three great Parisian essayists—were they and we to come face to face, how is it possible but that the right understanding would ensue?

A THOUGHT ON SHAKSPERE

From November Boughs (Philadelphia, 1888).

THE most distinctive poems—the most permanently rooted and with heartiest reason for being —the copious cycle of Arthurian legends, or the almost equally copious Charlemagne cycle, or the poems of the Cid, or Scandinavian Eddas, or Nibelungen, or Chaucer, or Spenser, or *bona fide* Ossian, or Inferno—probably had their rise in the great historic perturbations, which they came in to sum up and confirm, indirectly embodying results to date. Then however precious to "culture," the grandest of those poems, it may be said, preserve and typify results offensive to the modern spirit, and long passed away. To state it briefly, and taking the strongest examples, in Homer lives the ruthless military prowess of Greece, and of its special god-descended dynastic houses; in Shakspere the dragon-rancors and stormy feudal splendor of mediæval caste.

A THOUGHT ON SHAKSPERE

Poetry, largely consider'd, is an evolution, sending out improved and ever-expanded types, —in one sense, the past, even the best of it necessarily giving place, and dying out. For our existing world, the bases on which all the grand old poems were built have become vacuums—and even those of many comparatively modern ones are broken and half gone. For us to-day, not their own intrinsic value, vast as that is, backs and maintains those poems—but a mountain-high growth of associations, the layers of successive ages. Everywhere—their own lands included —(is there not something terrible in the tenacity with which the one book out of millions holds its grip?)—the. Homeric and Virgilian works, the interminable ballad-romances of the Middle Ages, the utterances of Dante, Spenser, and others, are upheld by their cumulus-entrenchment in scholarship, and as precious, always welcome, unspeakably valuable reminiscences.

Even the one who at present reigns unquestion'd—Shakspere—for all he stands for so much in modern literature, he stands entirely for the mighty æsthetic sceptres of the past, not for the spiritual and democratic, the sceptres of the future. The inward and outward characteristics of Shakspere are his vast and rich variety of persons and themes, with his wondrous delineation of each and all—not only limitless funds of verbal and pictorial resource, but great excess, superfœtation—mannerism, like a fine, aristocratic perfume, holding a touch of musk (Euphues, his mark)—with boundless sumptuousness and adornment, real velvet and gems, not shoddy nor paste—but a good deal of bombast and fustian—(certainly some terrific mouthing in Shakspere!)

Superb and inimitable as all is, it is mostly an objective and physiological kind of power and beauty the soul finds in Shakspere—a style supremely grand of the sort, but in my opinion stopping short of the grandest sort, at any rate for fulfilling and satisfying modern and scientific and democratic American purposes. Think, not of growths as forests primeval, or Yellowstone geysers, or Colorado ravines, but of costly marble palaces, and palace rooms, and the noblest fixings and furniture, and noble owners and occupants

[64]

to correspond—think of carefully built gardens from the beautiful but sophisticated gardening art at its best, with walks and bowers and artificial lakes, and appropriate statue-groups and the finest cultivated roses and lilies and japonicas in plenty—and you have the tally of Shakspere. The low characters, mechanics, even the loyal henchmen—all in themselves nothing—serve as capital foils to the aristocracy. The comedies (exquisite as they certainly are) bringing in admirably portray'd common characters, have the unmistakable hue of plays, portraits, made for the divertisement only of the élite of the castle, and from its point of view. The comedies are altogether non-acceptable to America and Democracy.

But to the deepest soul, it seems a shame to pick and choose from the riches Shakspere has left us—to criticise his infinitely royal, multiform quality—to gauge, with optic glasses, the dazzle of his sun-like beams.

The best poetic utterance, after all, can merely hint, or remind, often very indirectly, or at distant removes. Aught of real perfection, or the solution of any deep problem, or any completed statement of the moral, the true, the beautiful, eludes the greatest, deftest poet—flies away like an uncaught bird.

WHAT LURKS BEHIND SHAKSPERE'S HISTORICAL PLAYS?

From November Boughs (Philadelphia, 1888).

WE all know how much *mythus* there is in the Shakspere question as it stands to-day. Beneath a few foundations of proved facts are certainly engulf'd far more dim and elusive ones, of deepest importance—tantalizing and half suspected—suggesting explanations that one dare not put in plain statement. But coming at once to the point, the English historical plays are to me not only the most eminent as dramatic performances (my maturest judgment confirming the impression of my early years, that the distinctiveness and glory of the Poet reside not in his vaunted dramas of the passions, but those founded on the contests of English dynasties, and the French wars) but form, as we get it all, the chief in a complexity of puzzles. Conceiv'd out

of the fullest heat and pulse of European feudalism—personifying in unparallel'd ways the
mediæval aristocracy, its towering spirit of ruthless and gigantic caste, with its own peculiar air
and arrogance (no mere imitation)—only one of
the "wolfish earls" so plenteous in the plays themselves, or some born descendant and knower,
might seem to be the true author of those amazing works—works in some respects greater than
anything else in recorded literature.

The start and germ-stock of the pieces on
which the present speculation is founded are undoubtedly (with, at the outset, no small amount
of bungling work) in "Henry VI." It is plain
to me that as profound and forecasting a brain
and pen as ever appear'd in literature, after
floundering somewhat in the first part of that
trilogy—or perhaps draughting it more or less
experimentally or by accident—afterward developed and defined his plan in the Second and
Third Parts, and from time to time, thence forward, systematically enlarged it to majestic and
mature proportions in "Richard II," "Richard
III," "King John," "Henry IV," "Henry V," and

[68]

even in "Macbeth," "Coriolanus" and "Lear."
For it is impossible to grasp the whole cluster of
those plays, however wide the intervals and different circumstances of their composition, without thinking of them as, in a free sense, the
result of an *essentially controlling plan.* What
was that plan? Or, rather, what was veil'd behind it?—for to me there was certainly something so veil'd. Even the episodes of Cade,
Joan of Arc, and the like (which sometimes
seem to me like interpolations allow'd,) may
be meant to foil the possible sleuth, and throw
any too cute pursuer off the scent. In the
whole matter I should specially dwell on, and
make much of, that inexplicable element of every
highest poetic nature which causes it to cover up
and involve its real purpose and meanings in
folded removes and far recesses. Of this trait—
hiding the nest where common seekers may never
find it—the Shaksperean works afford the most
numerous and mark'd illustrations known to me.
I would even call that trait the leading one
through the whole of those works.

All the foregoing to premise a brief statement

[69]

of how and where I get my new light on Shakspere. Speaking of the special English plays, my
friend William O'Connor says:

They seem simply and rudely historical in their
motive, as aiming to give in the rough a tableau of
warring dynasties,—and carry to me a lurking sense
of being in aid of some ulterior design, probably
well enough understood in that age, which perhaps
time and criticism will reveal. . . . Their atmosphere
is one of barbarous and tumultuous gloom,—they do
not make us love the times they limn, . . . and it is
impossible to believe that the greatest of the Eliz-
abethan men could have sought to indoctrinate the
age with the love of feudalism which his own drama
in its entirety, if the view taken of it herein be true,
certainly and subtly saps and mines.

Reading the just-specified play in the light of
Mr. O'Connor's suggestion, I defy any one to
escape such new and deep utterance-meanings,
like magic ink, warm'd by the fire, and pre-
viously invisible. Will it not indeed be strange if
the author of "Othello" and "Hamlet" is destin'd
to live in America, in a generation or two, less as
the cunning draughtsman of the passions, and

[70]

more as putting on record the first full exposé—
and by far the most vivid one, immeasurably
ahead of doctrinaires and economists—of the
political theory and results, or the reason-why
and necessity for them which America has come
on earth to abnegate and replace?

The summary of my suggestion would be,
therefore, that while the more rich and tangled
jungle of the Shaksperean area is travers'd and
studied, and the more baffled and mix'd, as so far
appears, becomes the exploring student (who at
last surmises everything, and remains certain of
nothing) it is possible a future age of criticism,
diving deeper, mapping the land and lines freer,
completer than hitherto, may discover in the
plays named the scientific (Baconian?) inaugura-
tion of modern Democracy—furnishing realistic
and first-class artistic portraitures of the
mediæval world, the feudal personalties, institutes, in their morbid accumulations, deposits,
upon politics and sociology—may penetrate to
that hard-pan, far down and back of the ostent
of to-day, on which (and on which only) the
progressism of the last two centuries has built

RIVULETS OF PROSE

this Democracy which now holds secure lodgment over the whole civilized world.

Whether such was the unconscious, or (as I think likely) the more or less conscious, purpose of him who fashion'd those marvellous architectonics, is a secondary question.

ROBERT BURNS AS POET AND PERSON

From November Boughs (Philadelphia, 1888).

WHAT the future will decide about Robert Burns and his works—what place will be assign'd them on that great roster of geniuses and genius which can only be finish'd by the slow but sure balancing of the centuries with their ample average—I of course cannot tell. But as we know him, from his recorded utterances, and after nearly one century, and its diligence of collections, songs, letters, anecdotes, presenting the figure of the canny Scotchman in a fullness and detail wonderfully complete, and the lines mainly by his own hand, he forms to-day, in some respects, the most interesting personality among singers. Then there are many things in Burns's poems and character that specially endear him to America. He was essentially a Republican— would have been at home in the Western United

States, and probably become eminent there. He was an average sample of the good-natured, warm-blooded, proud-spirited, amative, alimentive, convivial, young and early-middle-aged man of the decent-born middle classes everywhere and any how. Without the race of which he is a distinct specimen, (and perhaps his poems) America and her powerful Democracy could not exist to-day—could not project with unparallel'd historic sway into the future.

Perhaps the peculiar coloring of the era of Burns needs always first to be consider'd. It included the times of the '76–'83 Revolution in America, of the French Revolution, and an unparallel'd chaos development in Europe and elsewhere. In every department, shining and strange names, like stars, some rising, some in meridian, some declining—Voltaire, Franklin, Washington, Kant, Goethe, Fulton, Napoleon, mark the era. And while so much, and of grandest moment, fit for the trumpet of the world's fame, was being transacted—that little tragi-comedy of R. B.'s life and death was going on in a country by-place in Scotland!

ROBERT BURNS AS POET AND PERSON

Burns's correspondence, generally collected and publish'd since his death, gives wonderful glints into both the amiable and weak (and worse than weak) parts of his portraiture, habits, good and bad luck, ambition and associations. His letters to Mrs. Dunlop, Mrs. McLehose, (Claninda,) Mr. Thompson, Dr. Moore, Robert Muir, Mr. Cunningham, Miss Margaret Chalmers, Peter Hill, Richard Brown, Mrs. Riddle, Robert Ainslie, and Robert Graham, afford valuable lights and shades to the outline, and with numerous others, help to a touch here, and fill-in there, of poet and poems. There are suspicions, it is true, of "the Genteel Letter Writer," with scraps and words from "the Manual of French Quotations," and, in the love-letters, some hollow mouthings. Yet we wouldn't on any account lack the letters. A full and true portrait is always what is wanted; veracity at every hazard. Besides, do we not all see by this time that the story of Burns, even for its own sake, requires the record of the whole and several, with nothing left out? Completely and every point minutely told out its fullest, explains and justifies itself—(as perhaps almost any life does). He is very close to the earth. He pick'd up his best words and tunes directly from the Scotch home-singers, but tells Thompson they would not please his, T's, "learn'd lugs," adding, "I call them simple—you would pronounce them silly." Yes, indeed; the idiom was undoubtedly his happiest hit. Yet Dr. Moore, in 1789, writes to Burns, "If I were to offer an opinion, it would be that in your future productions you should abandon the Scotch stanza and dialect, and adopt the measure and language of modern English poetry!"

As the 128th birth-anniversary of the poet draws on, (January, 1887,) with its increasing club-suppers, vehement celebrations, letters, speeches, and so on—(mostly, as William O'Connor says, from people who would not have noticed R. B. at all during his actual life, nor kept his company, or read his verses, on any account)—it may be opportune to print some leisurely-jotted notes I find in my budget. I take my observation of the Scottish bard by considering him as an individual amid the crowded clusters, galaxies, of the Old World—and fairly in-

ROBERT BURNS AS POET AND PERSON

quiring and suggesting what out of these myriads he too may be to the Western Republic. In the first place no poet on record so fully bequeaths his own personal magnetism,[1] nor illustrates more pointedly how one's verses, by time and reading, can curiously fuse with the versifier's own life and death, and give final light and shade to all.

I would say a large part of the fascination of Burns's homely, simple dialect-melodies is due, for all current and future readers, to the poet's personal "errors," the general bleakness of his lot, his ingrain'd pensiveness, his brief dash into dazzling, tantalizing, evanescent sunshine—fi-

---

[1] Probably no man that ever lived—a friend has made the statement—was so fondly loved, both by men and women, as Robert Burns. The reason is not hard to find: he had a real heart of flesh and blood beating in his bosom; you could almost hear it throb. "Some one said, that if you had shaken hands with him his hand would have burnt yours. The gods, indeed, made him poetical, but Nature had a hand in him first. His heart was in the right place; he did not pile up cantos of poetic diction; he pluck'd the mountain daisy under his feet; he wrote of field-mouse hurrying from its ruin'd dwelling. He held the plough or the pen with the same firm, manly grasp. And he was loved. The simple roll of the women who gave him their affection and their sympathy would make a long manuscript; and most of these were of such noble worth that, as Robert Chambers says, 'their character may stand as a testimony in favor of that of Burns.'" [As I understand, the foregoing is from an extremely rare book publish'd by M'Kie, in Kilmarnock. I find the whole beautiful paragraph in a capital paper on Burns, by Amelia Barr.]

nally culminating in those last years of his life, his being taboo'd and in debt, sick and sore, yaw'd as by contending gales, deeply dissatisfied with everything, most of all with himself—high-spirited too—(no man ever really higher-spirited than Robert Burns). I think it a perfectly legitimate part too. At any rate it has come to be an impalpable aroma through which only both the songs and their singer must henceforth be read and absorb'd. Through that view-medium of misfortune—of a noble spirit in low environments, and of a squalid and premature death—we view the undoubted facts, (giving, as we read them now, a sad kind of pungency,) that Burns's were, before all else, the lyrics of illicit loves and carousing intoxication. Perhaps even it is this strange, impalpable *post-mortem* comment and influence referr'd to, that gives them their contrast, attraction, making the zest of their author's after fame. If he had lived steady, fat, moral, comfortable, well-to-do years, on his own grade, (let alone, what of course was out of the question, the ease and velvet and rosewood and copious royalties of Tennyson or Victor

Hugo or Longfellow,) and died well-ripen'd and respectable, where could have come in that burst of passionate sobbing and remorse which well'd forth instantly and generally in Scotland, and soon follow'd everywhere among English-speaking races, on the announcement of his death? and which, with no sign of stopping, only regulated and vein'd with fitting appreciation, flows deeply, widely yet?

Dear Rob! manly, witty, fond, friendly, full of weak spots as well as strong ones—essential type of so many thousands—perhaps the average, as just said, of the decent-born young men and the early mid-aged, not only of the British Isles, but America, too, North and South, just the same. I think, indeed, one best part of Burns is the unquestionable proof he presents of the perennial existence among the laboring classes, especially farmers, of the finest latent poetic elements in their blood. (How clear it is to me that the common soil has always been, and is now, thickly strewn with just such gems.) He is well-called the *Ploughman*. "Holding the plough," said his brother Gilbert, "was the favor-

ite situation with Robert for poetic compositions; and some of his best verses were produced
while he was at that exercise." "I must return
to my humble station, and woo my rustic muse
in my wonted way, at the plough-tail." 1787, to
the Earl of Buchan. He has no high ideal of the
poet or the poet's office; indeed quite a low and
contracted notion of both:

> "Fortune! if thou'll but gie me still
> Hale breeks, a scone, and whiskey gill,
> An' rowth o'rhyme to rave at will,
> Tak' a' the rest."

See also his rhym'd letters to Robert Graham
invoking patronage; "one stronghold," Lord
Glencairn, being dead, now these appeals to "Fin-
tra, my other stay," (with in one letter a copious
shower of vituperation generally). In his collected poems there is no particular unity, nothing that can be called a leading theory, no unmistakable spine or skeleton. Perhaps, indeed, their
very desultoriness is the charm of his songs: "I
take up one or another," he says in a letter to

ROBERT BURNS AS POET AND PERSON

Thompson, "just as the bee of the moment buzzes in my bonnet-lug."

Consonantly with the customs of the time—yet markedly inconsistent in spirit with Burns's own case, (and not a little painful as it remains on record, as depicting some features of the bard himself,) the relation called *patronage* existed between the nobility and gentry on one side, and literary people on the other, and gives one of the strongest side-lights to the general coloring of poems and poets. It crops out a good deal in Burns's Letters, and even necessitated a certain flunkeyism on occasions, through life. It probably, with its requirements, (while it help'd in money and countenance) did as much as any one cause in making that life a chafed and unhappy one, ended by a premature and miserable death.

Yes, there is something about Burns peculiarly acceptable to the concrete, human points of view. He poetizes work-a-day agricultural labor and life, (whose spirit and sympathies, as well as practicalities, are much the same everywhere,) and treats fresh, often coarse, natural occurrences, loves, persons, not like many new and some old poets in a genteel style of gilt and china, or at second or third removes, but in their own born atmosphere, laughter, sweat, unction. Perhaps no one ever sang "lads and lasses"—that universal race, mainly the same, too, all ages, all lands—down on their own plane, as he has. He exhibits no philosophy worth mentioning; his morality is hardly more than parrot-talk—not bad or deficient, but cheap, shopworn, the platitudes of old aunts and uncles to the youngsters (be good boys and keep your noses clean). Only when he gets at Poosie Nansie's, celebrating the "barley bree," or among tramps, or democratic bouts and drinking generally,

("Freedom and whiskey gang thegither,")

we have, in his own unmistakable color and warmth, those interiors of rake-helly life and tavern fun—the cantabile of jolly beggars in highest jinks—lights and groupings of rank glee and brawny amorousness, outvying the best painted pictures of the Dutch school, or any school.

ROBERT BURNS AS POET AND PERSON

By America and her democracy such a poet, I cannot too often repeat, must be kept in loving remembrance; but it is best that discriminations be made. His admirers (as at those anniversary suppers, over the "hot Scotch") will not accept for their favorite anything less than the highest rank, alongside of Homer, Shakspere, etc. Such, in candor, are not the true friends of the Ayrshire bard, who really needs a different place quite by himself. The Iliad and the Odyssey express courage, craft, full-grown heroism in situations of danger, the sense of command and leadership, emulation, the last and fullest evolution of self-poise as in kings, and god-like even while animal appetites. The Shaksperean compositions, on vertebers and framework of the primary passions, portray (essentially the same as Homer's,) the spirit and letter of the feudal world, the Norman lord, ambitious and arrogant, taller and nobler than common men—with much underplay and gusts of heat and cold, volcanoes and stormy seas. Burns (and some will say to his credit) attempts none of these themes. He poetizes the humor, riotous blood, sulks, amorous

[83]

torments, fondness for the tavern and for cheap objective nature, with disgust at the grim and narrow ecclesiasticism of his time and land, of a young farmer on a bleak and hired farm in Scotland, through the years and under the circumstances of the British politics of that time, and of his short personal career as author, from 1783 to 1796. He is intuitive and affectionate, and just emerged or emerging from the shackles of the kirk, from poverty, ignorance, and from his own rank appetites—(out of which latter, however, he never extricated himself). It is to be said that amid not a little smoke and gas in his poems, there is in almost every piece a spark of fire, and now and then the real afflatus. He has been applauded as democratic, and with some warrant; while Shakspere, and with the greatest warrant, has been called monarchical or aristocratic (which he certainly is). But the splendid personalizations of Shakspere, formulated on the largest, freest, most heroic, most artistic mould, are to me far dearer as lessons, and more precious even as models for Democracy, than the humdrum samples Burns presents. The motives of

some of his effusions are certainly discreditable
personally—one or two of them markedly so. He
has, moreover, little or no spirituality. This last
is his mortal flaw and defect, tried by highest
standards. The ideal he never reach'd (and yet I
think he leads the way to it). He gives melodies,
and now and then the simplest and sweetest ones;
but harmonies, complications, oratorios in words,
never. (I do not speak this in any deprecatory
sense. Blessed be the memory of the warm-
hearted Scotchman for what he has left us, just
as it is!) He likewise did not know himself, in
more ways than one. Though so really free and
independent, he prided himself in his songs on
being a reactionist and a Jacobite—on persistent
sentimental adherency to the cause of the Stuarts
—the weakest, thinnest, most faithless, brain-
less dynasty that ever held a throne.

Thus, while Burns is not at all great for New
World study, in the sense that Isaiah and Eschylus and the book of Job are unquestionably great
—is not to be mention'd with Shakspere—hardly
even with current Tennyson or our Emerson—
he has a nestling niche of his own, all fragrant,

[85]

fond, and quaint and homely—a lodge built near but outside the mighty temple of the gods of song and art—those universal strivers, through their works of harmony and melody and power, to ever show or intimate man's crowning, last, victorious fusion in himself of Real and Ideal. Precious, too—fit and precious beyond all singers, high or low—will Burns ever be to the native Scotch, especially to the working-classes of North Britain; so intensely one of them, and so racy of the soil, sights, and local customs. He often apostrophizes Scotland, and is, or would be, enthusiastically patriotic. His country has lately commemorated him in a statue.[1] His aim is declaredly to be "a Rustic Bard." His poems were all written in youth or young manhood, (he was

[1] The Dumfries statue of Robert Burns was successfully unveil'd April 1881 by Lord Roseberry, the occasion having been made national in its character. Before the ceremony, a large procession paraded the streets of the town, all the trades and societies of that part of Scotland being represented, at the head of which went dairymen and ploughmen, the former driving their carts and being accompanied by their maids. The statue is of Sicilian marble. It rests on a pedestal of gray stone five feet high. The poet is represented as sitting easily on an old tree root, holding in his left hand a cluster of daisies. His face is turn'd toward the right shoulder, and the eyes gaze into the distance. Near by lie a collie dog, a broad bonnet half covering a well-thumb'd song-book, and a rustic flageolet. The costume is taken from the Nasmyth portrait, which has been follow'd for the features of the face.

ROBERT BURNS AS POET AND PERSON

little more than a young man when he died). His
collected works in giving everything, are nearly
one half first drafts. His brightest hit is his use of
the Scotch patois, so full of terms flavor'd like
wild fruits or berries. Then I should make an al-
lowance to Burns which cannot be made for any
other poet. Curiously even the frequent crudeness, haste, deficiencies, (flatness and puerilities
by no means absent) prove upon the whole not
out of keeping in any comprehensive collection
of his works, heroically printed, "following
copy," every piece, every line according to origi-
nals. Other poets might tremble for such bold-
ness, such rawness. In "this odd-kind chiel" such
points hardly mar the rest. Not only are they in
consonance with the underlying spirit of the
pieces, but complete the full abandon and veracity of the farm-fields and the home-brew'd
flavor of the Scotch vernacular. (Is there not
often something in the very neglect, unfinish,
careless nudity, slovenly hiatus, coming from intrinsic genius, and not "put on," that secretly
pleases the soul more than the wrought and re-
wrought polish of the most perfect verse?) Mark

the native spice and untranslatable twang in the very names of his songs—"O for ane and twenty, Tam," "John Barleycorn," "Last May a braw Wooer," "Rattlin roarin Willie," "O wert thou in the cauld, cauld blast," "Gude e'en to you, Kimmer," "Merry hae I been teething a Heckle," "O lay thy loof in mine, lass," and others.

The longer and more elaborated poems of Burns are just such as would please a natural but homely taste, and cute but average intellect, and are inimitable in their way. The "Twa Dogs," (one of the best) with the conversation between Cesar and Luath, the "Brigs of Ayr," "the Cotter's Saturday Night," "Tam O'Shanter"—all will be long read and re-read and admired, and ever deserve to be. With nothing profound in any of them, what there is of moral and plot has an inimitably fresh and racy flavor. If it came to question, Literature could well afford to send adrift many a pretensive poem, and even book of poems, before it could spare these compositions.

Never indeed was there truer utterance in a

certain range of idiosyncrasy than by this poet. Hardly a piece of his, large or small, but has "snap" and raciness. He puts in cantering rhyme (often doggerel) much cutting irony and idiomatic ear-cuffing of the kirk-deacons—drily good-natured addresses to his cronies, (he certainly would not stop us if he were here this moment, from classing that "to the De'il" among them)—"to Mailie and her Lambs," "to auld Mare Maggie," "to a Mouse,"

"Wee, sleekit, cowrin, tim'rous beastie":

"to a Mountain Daisy," "to a Haggis," "to a Louse," "to the Toothache," etc.— and occasionally to his brother bards and lady or gentleman patrons, often with strokes of tenderest sensibility, idiopathic humor, and genuine poetic imagination—still oftener with shrewd, original, sheeny, steel-flashes of wit, home-spun sense, or lance-blade puncturing. Then, strangely, the basis of Burns's character, with all its fun and manliness, was hypochondria, the blues, palpable enough in "Despondency," "Man was made to

[89]

Mourn," "Address to Ruin," a "Bard's Epitaph,"
&c. From such deep-down elements sprout up,
in very contrast and paradox, those riant utterances of which a superficial reading will not detect the hidden foundation. Yet nothing is clearer
to me than the black and desperate background
behind those pieces—as I shall now specify them.
I find his most characteristic, Nature's masterly
touch and luxuriant life-blood, color and heat,
not in "Tam O'Shanter," "the Cotter's Saturday
Night," "Scots wha hae," "Highland Mary,"
"the Twa Dogs," and the like, but in "the Jolly
Beggars," "Rigs of Barley," "Scotch Drink,"
"the Epistle to John Rankine," "Holy Willie's
Prayer," and in "Halloween," (to say nothing
of a certain cluster, known still to a small inner
circle in Scotland, but, for good reasons, not
published anywhere). In these compositions,
especially the first, there is much indelicacy
(some editions flatly leave it out,) but the com-
poser reigns alone, with handling free and broad
and true, and is an artist. You may see and feel
the man indirectly in his other verses, all of them,
with more or less life-likeness—but these I have

named last call out pronouncedly in his own voice,

"I, Rob, am here."

Finally, in any summing-up of Burns, though so much is to be said in the way of fault-finding, drawing black marks, and doubtless severe literary criticism—(in the present outpouring I have "kept myself in," rather than allow'd any free flow)—after full retrospect of his works and life, the aforesaid "odd-kind chiel" remains to my heart and brain as almost the tenderest, manliest, and (even if contradictory) dearest flesh-and-blood figure in all the streams and clusters of bygone poets.

A WORD ABOUT TENNYSON

From November Boughs (Philadelphia, 1888).

BEAUTIFUL as the song was, the original "Locks-ley Hall" of half a century ago was essentially morbid, heart-broken, finding fault with every-thing, especially the fact of money's being made (as it ever must be, and perhaps should be) the paramount matter in worldly affairs;

Every door is barr'd with gold, and opens but to golden keys.

First, a father, having fallen in battle, his child (the singer)

Was left a trampled orphan, and a selfish uncle's ward.

Of course love ensues. The woman in the chant or monologue proves a false one; and as far as appears the ideal of woman, in the poet's reflec-tions, is a false one—at any rate for America. Woman is *not* "the lesser man." (The heart is

[92]

A WORD ABOUT TENNYSON

not the brain.) The best of the piece of fifty years since is its concluding line:

For the mighty wind arises roaring seaward and I go.

Then for this current 1886–7, a just-out sequel, which (as an apparently authentic summary says) "reviews the life of mankind during the past sixty years, comes to the conclusion that its boasted progress is of doubtful credit to the world in general and to England in particular. A cynical vein of denunciation of democratic opinions and aspirations runs throughout the poem in mark'd contrast with the spirit of the poet's youth." Among the most striking lines of this sequel are the following:

Envy wears the mask of love, and, laughing sober fact
　　to scorn,
Cries to weakest as to strongest, "Ye are equals, equal
　　born,"
Equal-born! Oh, yes, if yonder hill be level with
　　the flat.
Charm us, orator, till the lion look no larger than
　　the cat:
Till the cat, through that mirage of overheated lan-
　　guage, loom

[93]

Larger than the lion Demo—end in working its
   own doom.
Tumble Nature heel o'er head, and, yelling with the
   yelling street,
Set the feet above the brain, and swear the brain
   is in the feet.
Bring the old dark ages back, without the faith, without the hope
Beneath the State, the Church, the Throne, and roll
   their ruins down the slope.

I should say that all this is a legitimate conse-
quence of the tone and convictions of the earlier
standards and points of view. Then some reflec-
tions, down to the hard-pan of this sort of thing.

The course of progressive politics (democracy) is so certain and resistless, not only in
America but in Europe, that we can well afford
the warning calls, threats, checks, neutralizings,
in imaginative literature, or any department, of
such deep-sounding and high-soaring voices as
Carlyle's and Tennyson's. Nay, the blindness, excesses, of the prevalent tendency—the dangers of
the urgent trends of our times—in my opinion,
need such voices almost more than any. I should,
too, call it a signal instance of democratic hu-

A WORD ABOUT TENNYSON

manity's luck that it has such enemies to contend
with—so candid, so fervid, so heroic. But why
do I say enemies? Upon the whole is not Tennyson—and was not Carlyle (like an honest and
stern physician)—the true friend of our age?

Let me assume to pass verdict, or perhaps
momentary judgment, for the United States on
this poet—a remov'd and distant position giving
some advantages over a nigh one. What is Tennyson's service to his race, times and especially
to America? First, I should say—or at least not
forget—his personal character. He is not to be
mention'd as a rugged, evolutionary, aboriginal
force—but (and a great lesson is in it) he has
been consistent throughout with the native,
healthy, patriotic spinal element and promptings
of himself. His moral line is local and conventional, but it is vital and genuine. He reflects the
upper-crust of his time, its pale cast of thought—
even its *ennui*. Then the simile of my friend John
Burroughs is entirely true, "his glove is a glove
of silk, but the hand is a hand of iron." He shows
how one can be a royal laureate, quite elegant and
"aristocratic," and a little queer and affected,

and at the same time perfectly manly and natural. As to his non-democracy, it fits him well,
and I like him the better for it. I guess we all like
to have (I am sure I do) some one who presents
those sides of a thought, or possibility, different
from our own—different and yet with a sort of
home-likeness—a tartness and contradiction offsetting the theory as we view it, and construed
from tastes and proclivities not at all his own.

To me, Tennyson shows more than any poet
I know (perhaps has been a warning to me) how
much there is in finest verbalism. There is such
a latent charm in mere words, cunning collocu-
tions, and in the voice ringing them, which he
has caught and brought out, beyond all others
—as in the line,

And hollow, hollow, hollow, all delight,

in "The Passing of Arthur," and evidenced in
"The Lady of Shalott," "The Deserted House,"
and many other pieces. Among the best (I often
linger over them again and again) are "Lucretius," "The Lotos Eaters," and "The Northern
Farmer." His mannerism is great, but it is a

noble and welcome mannerism. His very best work, to me, is contain'd in the books of "The Idyls of the King," and all that has grown out of them. Though indeed we could spare nothing of Tennyson, however small or however peculiar —not "Break, Break," nor "Flower in the Crannied Wall," nor the old, eternally-told passion of "Edward Gray":

> Love may come and love may go,
>   And fly like a bird from tree to tree.
> But I will love no more, no more
>   Till Ellen Adair come back to me.

Yes, Alfred Tennyson's is a superb character, and will help give illustriousness, through the long roll of time, to our Nineteenth Century. In its bunch of orbic names, shining like a constellation of stars, his will be one of the brightest. His very faults, doubts, swervings, doublings upon himself, have been typical of our age. We are like the voyagers of a ship, casting off for new seas, distant shores. We would still dwell in the old suffocating and dead haunts, remembering and magnifying their pleasant ex-

periences only, and more than once impell'd to
jump ashore before it is too late, and stay where
our fathers stay'd, and live as they lived.

May-be I am non-literary and non-decorous
(let me at least be human, and pay part of
my debt) in this word about Tennyson. I want
him to realize that here is a great and ardent
Nation that absorbs his songs, and has a respect
and affection for him personally, as almost for no
other foreigner. I want this word to go to the
old man at Farringford as conveying no more
than the simple truth; and that truth (a little
Christmas gift) no slight one either. I have written impromptu, and shall let it all go at that.
The readers of more than fifty millions of people
in the New World not only owe to him some of
their most agreeable and harmless and healthy
hours, but he has enter'd into the formative influences of character here, not only in the
Atlantic cities, but inland and far West, out in
Missouri, in Kansas, and away in Oregon, in
farmer's house and miner's cabin.

Best thanks, anyhow, to Alfred Tennyson—
thanks and appreciation in America's name.

OLD POETS

From Good-Bye My Fancy (Philadelphia, 1891).

POETRY (I am clear) is eligible of something far more ripen'd and ample, our lands and pending days, than it has yet produced from any utterance old or new. Modern or new poetry, too, (viewing or challenging it with severe criticism,) is largely a void—while the very cognizance, or even suspicion of that void, and the need of filling it, proves a certainty of the hidden and waiting supply. Leaving other lands and languages to speak for themselves, we can abruptly but deeply suggest it best from our own—going first to oversea illustrations, and standing on them. Think of Byron, Burns, Shelley, Keats, (even first-raters, "the brothers of the radiant summit," as William O'Connor calls them,) as having done only their precursory and 'prentice work, and all their best and real poems being left

[99]

yet unwrought, untouch'd. Is it difficult to imagine ahead of us and them, evolv'd from them,
poesy completer far than any they themselves
fulfill'd? One has in his eye and mind some very
large, very old, entirely sound and vital tree or
vine, like certain hardy, ever-fruitful specimens
in California and Canada, or down in Mexico,
(and indeed in all lands,) beyond the chronolog-
ical records—illustrations of growth, continuity,
power, amplitude and *exploitation,* almost beyond statement, but proving fact and possibility,
outside of argument.

Perhaps, indeed, the rarest and most blessed
quality of transcendent noble poetry—as of law,
and of the profoundest wisdom and æstheticism
—is, (I would suggest,) from sane, completed,
vital, capable old age. The final proof of song or
personality is a sort of matured, accreted, superb,
evoluted, almost divine, impalpable diffuseness
and atmosphere or invisible magnetism, dissolving
and embracing all—and not any special achieve-
ment of passion, pride, metrical form, epigram,
plot, thought, or what is call'd beauty. The bud
of the rose or the half-blown flower is beautiful,

of course, but only the perfected bloom or apple or finish'd wheat-head is beyond the rest. Completed fruitage like this comes (in my opinion) to a grand age, in man or woman, through an essentially sound continuated physiology and psychology (both important) and is the culminating glorious aureole of all and several preceding. Like the tree or vine just mention'd, it stands at last in a beauty, power and productiveness of its own, above all others, and of a sort and style uniting all criticisms, proofs and adherences.

Let us diversify the matter a little by portraying some of the American poets from our own point of view.

Longfellow, reminiscent, polish'd, elegant, with the air of finest conventional library, picture-gallery or parlor, with ladies and gentlemen in them, and plush and rosewood, and ground-glass lamps, and mahogany and ebony furniture, and a silver inkstand and scented satin paper to write on.

Whittier stands for morality (not in any all-accepting philosophic or Hegelian sense, but)

filter'd through a Puritanical or Quaker filter—
is incalculably valuable as a genuine utterance,
(and the finest,)—with many local and Yankee
and *genre* bits—all hued with anti-slavery coloring—(the *genre* and anti-slavery contributions
all precious—all help). Whittier's is rather a
grand figure, but pretty lean and ascetic—no
Greek—not universal and composite enough
(don't try—don't wish to be) for ideal Americanism. Ideal Americanism would take the
Greek spirit and law, and democratize and
scientize and (thence) truly Christianize them
for the whole, the globe, all history, all ranks
and lands, all facts, all good and bad. (Ah this
bad—this nineteen-twentieths of us all! What
a stumbling-block it remains for poets and
metaphysicians—what a chance (the strange,
clear-as-ever inscriptions on the old dug-up
tablet) it offers yet for being translated—what
can be its purpose in the God-scheme of this
universe, and all?)

Then William Cullen Bryant—meditative,
serious, from first to last tending to threnodies

—his genius mainly lyrical—when reading his pieces who could expect or ask for more magnificent ones than such as "The Battle-Field," and "A Forest Hymn"? Bryant, unrolling, prairie-like, notwithstanding his mountains and lakes— moral enough (yet worldly and conventional) —a naturalist, pedestrian, gardener and fruiter —well aware of books, but mixing to the last in cities and society. I am not sure but his name ought to lead the list of American bards. Years ago I thought Emerson pre-eminent (and as to the last polish and intellectual cuteness may-be I think so still)—but, for reasons, I have been gradually tending to give the file-leading place for American native poesy to W. C. B.

Of Emerson I have to confirm my already avow'd opinion regarding his highest bardic and personal attitude. Of the galaxy of the past— of Poe, Halleck, Mrs. Sigourney, Allston, Willis, Dana, John Pierpont, W. G. Simms, Robert Sands, Drake, Hillhouse, Theodore Fay, Margaret Fuller, Epes Sargent, Boker, Paul Hayne, Lanier, and others, I fitly in essaying such a theme as this, and reverence for their memories, may at least give a heart-benison on the list of their names.

Time and New World humanity having the venerable resemblances more than anything else, and being "the same subject continued," just here in 1890, one gets a curious nourishment and lift (I do) from all those grand old veterans, Bancroft, Kossuth, von Moltke—and such typical specimen-reminiscences as Sophocles and Goethe, genius, health, beauty of person, riches, rank, renown and length of days, all combining and centering in one case.

Above everything, what could humanity and literature do without the mellow, past-justifying, averaging, bringing-up of many, many years—a great old age amplified? Every really first-class production has likely to pass through the crucial tests of a generation, perhaps several generations. Lord Bacon says the first sight of any work really new and first-rate in beauty and originality always arouses something disagreeable and repulsive. Voltaire term'd the Shaksperean works "a huge dunghill"; "Hamlet" he described (to the Academy, whose members listen'd with approbation) as "the dream of a drunken savage, with a few flashes of beautiful thoughts." And not the Ferney sage alone; the orthodox judges and law-givers of France, such as La Harpe, J. L. Geoffroy, and Chateaubriand, either join'd in Voltaire's verdict, or went further. Indeed the classicists and regulars there still hold to it. The lesson is very significant in all departments. People resent anything new as a personal insult. When umbrellas were first used in England, those who carried them were hooted and pelted so furiously that their lives were endanger'd. The same rage encounter'd the attempt in theatricals to perform women's parts by real women, which was publicly consider'd disgusting and outrageous. Byron thought Pope's verse incomparably ahead of Homer and Shakspere. One of the prevalent objections, in the days of Columbus was, the learn'd men boldly asserted that if a ship should reach India she would never get back again, because the rotundity of the globe would present a kind of mountain, up which it would be impossible to sail even with the most favorable wind.

"Modern poets," says a leading Boston journal, "enjoy longevity. Browning lived to be seventy-seven. Wordsworth, Bryant, Emerson, and Longfellow were old men. Whittier, Tennyson, and Walt Whitman still live." Started out by that item on Old Poets and Poetry for chyle to inner American sustenance—I have thus gossipp'd about it all, and treated it from my own point of view, taking the privilege of rambling wherever the talk carried me. Browning is lately dead; Bryant, Emerson and Longfellow have not long pass'd away; and, yes, Whittier and Tennyson remain, over eighty years old—the latter having sent out not long since a fresh volume, which the English-speaking Old and New Worlds are yet reading. I have already put on record my notions of T. and his effusions: they are very attractive and flowery to me—but flowers, too, are at least as profound as anything; and by common consent T. is settled as the poetic cream-skimmer of our age's melody, *ennui* and polish—

a verdict in which I agree, and should say that no-
body (not even Shakspere) goes deeper in those
exquisitely touch'd and half-hidden hints and
indirections left like faint perfumes in the
crevices of his lines. Of Browning I don't know
enough to say much; he must be studied deeply
out, too, and quite certainly repays the trouble
—but I am old and indolent, and cannot study
(and never did).

Grand as to-day's accumulative fund of poetry
is, there is certainly something unborn, not yet
come forth, different from anything now formulated in any verse, or contributed by the past
in any land—something waited for, craved,
hitherto non-express'd. What it will be, and how,
no one knows. It will probably have to prove itself by itself and its readers. One thing, it must
run through entire humanity (this new word and
meaning Solidarity has arisen to us moderns)
twining all lands like a divine thread, stringing
all beads, pebbles or gold, from God and the soul,
and like God's dynamics and sunshine illustrating
all and having reference to all. From anything
like a cosmical point of view, the entirety of

imaginative literature's themes and results as we get them to-day seems painfully narrow. All that has been put in statement, tremendous as it is, what is it compared with the vast fields and values and varieties left unreap'd? Of our own country, the splendid races North or South, and especially of the Western and Pacific regions, it sometimes seems to me their myriad noblest Homeric and Bible elements are all untouch'd, left as if ashamed of, and only certain very minor occasional *delirium tremens* glints studiously sought and put in print, in short tales, "poetry" or books.

I give these speculations, or notions, in all their audacity, for the comfort of thousands—perhaps a majority of ardent minds, women's and young men's—who stand in awe and despair before the immensity of suns and stars already in the firmament. Even in the Iliad and Shakspere there is (is there not?) a certain humiliation produced to us by the absorption of them, unless we sound in equality, or above them, the songs due our own democratic era and surroundings, and the fullest assertion of ourselves. And in vain (such is my opinion) will America seek successfully to tune any superb national song unless the heart-strings of the people start it from their own breasts—to be return'd and echoed there again.

AMERICAN NATIONAL LITERATURE

IS THERE ANY SUCH THING—OR CAN THERE EVER BE?

From Good-Bye My Fancy (Philadelphia, 1891).

So you want an essay about American National Literature, (tremendous and fearful subject!) do you? [1] Well, if you will let me put down some melanged cogitations regarding the matter, haphazard, and from my own points of view, I will try. Horace Greeley wrote a book named "Hints Toward Reforms," and the title-line was consider'd the best part of all. In the present case I will give a few thoughts and suggestions, of good and ambitious intent enough anyhow—first reiterating the question right out plainly: American National Literature—is there distinctively any such thing, or can there ever be? First to me

[1] The essay was for the *North American Review*, in answer to the formal request of the editor. It appear'd in March, 1891.

[110]

comes an almost indescribably august form, the People, with varied typical shapes and attitudes—then the divine mirror, Literature.

As things are, probably no more puzzling question ever offer'd itself than (going back to old Nile for a trope,) What bread-seeds of printed mentality shall we cast upon America's waters, to grow and return after many days? Is there for the future authorship of the United States any better way than submission to the teeming facts, events, activities, and importations already vital through and beneath them all? I have often ponder'd it, and felt myself disposed to let it go at that. Indeed, are not those facts and activities and importations potent and certain to fulfill themselves all through our Commonwealth, irrespective of any attempt from individual guidance? But allowing all, and even at that, a good part of the matter being honest discussion, examination, and earnest personal presentation, we may even for sanitary exercise and contact plunge boldly into the spread of the many waves and cross-tides, as follows. Or, to change the figure, I will present my varied little

[111]

collation (what is our Country itself but an infinitely vast and varied collation?) in the hope that the show itself indicates a duty getting more and more incumbent every day.

In general, civilization's totality or real representative National Literature formates itself (like language or "the weather") not from two or three influences, however important, nor from any learned syllabus, or criticism, or what ought to be, nor from any minds or advice of toploftical quarters—and indeed not at all from the influences and ways ostensibly supposed (though they too are adopted, after a sort)—but slowly, slowly, curiously, from many more and more, deeper mixings and siftings (especially in America) and generations and years and races, and what largely appears to be chance—but is not chance at all. First of all, for future National Literature in America, New England (the technically moral and schoolmaster region, as a cynical fellow I know calls it) and the three or four great Atlantic-coast cities, highly as they to-day suppose they dominate the whole, will have to haul in their horns. *Ensemble* is the taproot of National Literature. America is become already a huge world of peoples, rounded and orbic climates, idiocrasies, and geographies—forty-four Nations curiously and irresistibly blent and aggregated in ONE NATION, with one imperial language, and one unitary set of social and legal standards over all—and (I predict) a yet to be National Literature. (In my mind this last, if it ever comes, is to prove grander and more important for the Commonwealth than its politics and material wealth and trade, vast and indispensable as those are.)

Think a moment what must, beyond peradventure, be the real permanent sub-bases, or lack of them. Books profoundly consider'd show a great nation more than anything else—more than laws or manners. (This is, of course, probably the deep-down meaning of that well-buried but ever-vital platitude, Let me sing the people's songs, and I don't care who makes their laws.) Books too reflect humanity *en masse*, and surely show them splendidly, or the reverse, and prove or celebrate their prevalent traits (these last the main things.) Homer grew out of and has held

the ages, and holds to-day, by the universal admiration for personal prowess, courage, rankness,
amour propre, leadership, inherent in the whole
human race. Shakspere concentrates the bril-
liancy of the centuries of feudalism on the proud
personalities they produced, and paints the amorous passion. The books of the Bible stand for
the final superiority of devout emotions over the
rest, and of religious adoration, and ultimate absolute justice, more powerful than haughtiest
kings or millionaires or majorities.

What the United States are working out and
establishing needs imperatively the connivance
of something subtler than ballots and legislators.
The Goethean theory and lesson (if I may briefly
state it so) of the exclusive sufficiency of artistic,
scientific, literary equipment to the character,
irrespective of any strong claims of the political
ties of nation, state, or city, could have answer'd
under the conventionality and pettiness of
Weimar, or the Germany, or even Europe, of
those times; but it will not do for America to-
day at all. We have not only to exploit our own
theory above any that has preceded us, but we

have entirely different, and deeper-rooted, and infinitely broader themes.

When I have had a chance to see and observe a sufficient crowd of American boys or maturer youths or well-grown men, all the States, as in my experiences in the Secession War among the soldiers, or west, east, north, or south, or my wanderings and loiterings through cities (especially New York and in Washington,) I have invariably found coming to the front three prevailing personal traits, to be named here for brevity's sake under the heads Good-Nature, Decorum, and Intelligence. (I make Good-Nature first, as it deserves to be—it is a splendid resultant of all the rest, like health or fine weather.) Essentially these lead the inherent list of the high average personal born and bred qualities of the young fellows everywhere through the United States, as any sharp observer can find out for himself. Surely these make the vertebral stock of superbest and noblest nations! May the destinies show it so forthcoming. I mainly confide the whole future of our Commonwealth to the fact of these three bases, need

[115]

I say I demand the same, in the elements and spirit and fruitage of National Literature?

Another, perhaps a born root or branch, comes under the words *Noblesse Oblige*, even for a national rule or motto. My opinion is that this foregoing phrase, and its spirit, should influence and permeate official America and its representatives in Congress, the Executive Departments, the Presidency, and the individual States—should be one of their chiefest mottoes, and be carried out practically. (I got the idea from my dear friend the democratic Englishwoman, Mrs. Anne Gilchrist, now dead. "The beautiful words *Noblesse Oblige*," said she to me once, "are not best for some develop'd gentleman or lord, but some rich and develop'd nation—and especially for your America.")

Then another and very grave point (for this discussion is deep, deep—not for trifles, or pretty seemings.) I am not sure but the establish'd and old (and superb and profound, and, one may say, needed as old) conception of Deity as mainly of moral constituency (goodness, purity, sinlessness, &c.) has been undermined by nineteenth century ideas and science. What does this immense and almost abnormal development of Philanthropy mean among the moderns? One doubts if there ever will come a day when the moral laws and moral standards will be supplanted as over all: while time proceeds (I find it so myself) they will probably be intrench'd deeper and expanded wider. Then the expanded scientific and democratic and truly philosophic and poetic quality of modernism demands a Deific identity and scope superior to all limitations, and essentially including just as well the so-call'd evil and crime and criminals—all the malformations, the defective and abortions of the universe.

Sometimes the bulk of the common people (who are far more 'cute than the critics suppose) relish a well-hidden allusion or hint carelessly dropt, faintly indicated, and left to be disinterr'd or not. Some of the very old ballads have delicious morsels of this kind. Greek Aristophanes and Pindar abounded in them. (I sometimes fancy the old Hellenic audiences must have been as generally keen and knowing as any of their poets.) Shakspere is full of them. Tennyson has them. It is always a capital compliment from author to reader, and worthy the peering brains of America. The mere smartness of the common folks, however, does not need encouraging, but qualities more solid and opportune.

What are now deepest wanted in the States as roots for their literature are Patriotism, Nationality, Ensemble, or the ideas of these, and the uncompromising genesis and saturation of these. Not the mere bawling and braggadocio of them, but the radical emotion-facts, the fervor and perennial fructifying spirit at fountain-head. And at the risk of being misunderstood I should dwell on and repeat that a great imaginative *literatus* for America can never be merely good and moral in the conventional method. Puritanism and what radiates from it must always be mention'd by me with respect; then I should say, for this vast and varied Commonwealth, geographically and artistically, the puritanical standards are constipated, narrow, and non-philosophic.

In the main I adhere to my positions in "Democratic Vistas," and especially to my summing-up of American literature as far as to-day is concern'd. In Scientism, the Medical Profession, Practical Inventions, and Journalism, the United States have press'd forward to the glorious front rank of advanced civilized lands, as also in the popular dissemination of printed matter (of a superficial nature perhaps, but that is an indispensable preparatory stage,) and have gone in common education, so-call'd, far beyond any other land or age. Yet the high-pitch'd taunt of Margaret Fuller, forty years ago, still sounds in the air: "It does not follow, because the United States print and read more books, magazines, and newspapers than all the rest of the world, that they really have therefore a literature." For perhaps it is not alone the free schools and newspapers, nor railroads and factories, nor all the iron, cotton, wheat, pork, and petroleum, nor the gold and silver, nor the surplus of a hundred or several hundred millions, nor the Fourteenth and Fifteenth Amendments, nor the last national census, that can put this Commonweal high or highest on the cosmical scale of history.

Something else is indispensable. All that record is
lofty, but there is a loftier.

The great current points are perhaps simple,
after all: first, that the highest developments of
the New World and Democracy, and probably
the best society of the civilized world all over,
are to be only reach'd and spinally nourish'd (in
my notion) by a new evolutionary sense and
treatment; and, secondly, that the evolution-
principle, which is the greatest law through nature, and of course in these States, has now
reach'd us markedly for and in our literature.

In other writings I have tried to show how
vital to any aspiring Nationality must ever be
its autochthonic song, and how for a really great
people there can be no complete and glorious
Name, short of emerging out of and even rais'd
on such born poetic expression, coming from its
own soil and soul, its area, spread, idiosyncrasies,
and (like showers of rain, originally rising impalpably, distill'd from land and sea,) duly returning there again. Nor do I forget what we all
owe to our ancestry; though perhaps we are apt
to forgive and bear too much for that alone.

AMERICAN NATIONAL LITERATURE

One part of the national American literatus's task is (and it is not an easy one) to treat the old hereditaments, legends, poems, theologies, and even customs, with fitting respect and toleration, and at the same time clearly understand and justify, and be devoted to and exploit our own day, its diffused light, freedom, responsibilities, with all it necessitates, and that our New-World circumstances and stages of development demand and make proper. For American literature we want mighty authors, *not* even Carlyle- and Heine-like, born and brought up in (and more or less essentially partaking and giving out) that vast abnormal ward or hysterical sick-chamber which in many respects Europe, with all its glories, would seem to be. The greatest feature in current poetry (perhaps in literature anyhow) is the almost total lack of first-class power, and simple, natural health, flourishing and produced at first hand, typifying our own era. Modern verse generally lacks quite altogether the modern, and is oftener possess'd in spirit with the past and feudal, dressed may-be in late fashions. From novels and plays often the plots and surfaces are contemporary—but the spirit, even the fun, is morbid and effete.

There is an essential difference between the Old and New. The poems of Asia and Europe are rooted in the long past. They celebrate man and his intellections and relativenesses as they have been. But America, in as high a strain as ever, is to sing them all as they are and are to be. (I know, of course, that the past is probably a main factor in what we are and know and must be.) At present the States are absorb'd in business, money-making, politics, agriculture, the development of mines, inter-communications, and other material attents—which all show forward and appear at their height—as, consistently with modern civilization, they must be and should be. Then even these are but the inevitable precedents and providers for home-born, transcendent, democratic literature—to be shown in superior, more heroic, more spiritual, more emotional, personalities and songs. A national literature is, of course, in one sense, a great mirror or reflector. There must however be something before—something to reflect. I should say now, since the Secession War, there has been, and to-day unquestionably exists, that something.

Certainly, anyhow, the United States do not so far utter poetry, first-rate literature, or any of the so-call'd arts, to any lofty admiration or advantage—are not dominated or penetrated from actual inherence or plain bent to the said poetry and arts. Other work, other needs, current inventions, productions, have occupied and to-day mainly occupy them. They are very 'cute and imitative and proud—can't bear being left too glaringly away far behind the other high-class nations—and so we set up some home "poets," "artists," painters, musicians, *literati,* and so forth, all our own (thus claim'd). The whole matter has gone on, and exists to-day, probably as it should have been, and should be; as, for the present, it must be. To all which we conclude, and repeat the terrible query: American National Literature—is there distinctively any such thing, or can there ever be?

THE OLD BOWERY

A REMINISCENCE OF NEW YORK PLAYS AND ACTING FIFTY YEARS AGO

From November Boughs (Philadelphia, 1888).

IN an article not long since, "Mrs. Siddons as Lady Macbeth," in "The Nineteenth Century," after describing the bitter regretfulness to mankind from the loss of those first-class poems, temples, pictures, gone and vanish'd from any record of men, the writer (Fleeming Jenkin) continues:

If this be our feeling as to the more durable works of art, what shall we say of those triumphs which, by their very nature, last no longer than the action which creates them—the triumph of the orator, the singer or the actor? There is an anodyne in the words, "must be so," "inevitable," and there is even some absurdity in longing for the impossible. This anodyne and our sense of humor temper the unhappiness we feel when, after hearing some great performance, we leave the

[124]

THE OLD BOWERY

theatre and think, "Well, this great thing has been, and all that is now left of it is the feeble print upon my brain, the little thrill which memory will send along my nerves, mine and my neighbors', as we live longer the print and thrill must be feebler, and when we pass away the impress of the great artist will vanish from the world." The regret that a great art should in its nature be transitory, explains the lively interest which many feel in reading the anecdotes or descriptions of a great actor.

All this is emphatically my own feeling and reminiscence about the best dramatic and lyric artists I have seen in bygone days—for instance, Marietta Alboni, the elder Booth, Forrest, the tenor Bettini, the baritone Badiali, "old man Clarke"—(I could write a whole paper on the latter's peerless rendering of the Ghost in "Hamlet" at the Park, when I was a young fellow—an actor named Ranger, who appear'd in America forty years ago in *genre* characters; Henry Placide, and many others. But I will make a few memoranda at least of the best one I knew.

For the elderly New Yorker of to-day, perhaps, nothing were more likely to start up memories of his early manhood than the mention of the Bowery and the elder Booth. At the date given, the more stylish and select theatre (prices, 50 cents pit, $1 boxes) was "The Park," a large and well-appointed house on Park Row, opposite the present Post-office. English opera and the old comedies were often given in capital style; the principal foreign stars appear'd here, with Italian opera at wide intervals. The Park held a large part in my boyhood's and young manhood's life. Here I heard the English actor, Anderson, in "Charles de Moor," and in the fine part of "Gisippus." Here I heard Fanny Kemble, Charlotte Cushman, the Seguins, Daddy Rice, Hackett as Falstaff, Nimrod Wildfire, Rip Van Winkle, and in his Yankee characters. It was here (some years later than the date in the headlines) I also heard Mario many times, and at his best. In such parts as Gennaro, in "Lucrezia Borgia," he was inimitable—the sweetest of voices, a pure tenor, of considerable compass and respectable power. His wife, Grisi, was with him, no longer first-class or young—a fine Norma, though, to the last.

Perhaps my dearest amusement reminiscences are those musical ones. I doubt if ever the senses and emotions of the future will be thrill'd as were the auditors of a generation ago by the deep passion of Alboni's contralto (at the Broadway Theatre, south side, near Pearl street)—or by the trumpet notes of Badiali's baritone, or Bettini's pensive and incomparable tenor in Fernando in "Favorita," or Marini's bass in "Faliero," among the Havana troupe, Castle Garden.

But getting back more specifically to the date and theme I started from—the heavy tragedy business prevail'd more decidedly at the Bowery Theatre, where Booth and Forrest were frequently to be heard. Though Booth *père,* then in his prime, ranging in age from 40 to 44 years (he was born in 1796,) was the loyal child and continuer of the traditions of orthodox English playacting, he stood out "himself alone" in many respects beyond any of his kind on record, and with effects and ways that broke through all rules and all traditions. He has been well describ'd as an actor "whose instant and tremendous concentration of passion in his delineations overwhelm'd his audience, and wrought into it such enthusiasm that it partook of the fever of inspiration

[127]

surging through his own veins." He seems to have been of beautiful private character, very honorable, affectionate, good-natured, no arrogance, glad to give the other actors the best chances. He knew all stage points thoroughly, and curiously ignored the mere dignities. I once talk'd with a man who had seen him do the Second Actor in the mock play to Charles Kean's Hamlet in Baltimore. He was a marvellous linguist. He play'd Shylock once in London, giving the dialogue in Hebrew, and in New Orleans Oreste (Racine's "Andromaque") in French. One trait of his habits, I have heard, was strict vegetarianism. He was exceptionally kind to the brute creation. Every once in a while he would make a break for solitude or wild freedom, sometimes for a few hours, sometimes for days. (He illustrated Plato's rule that to the forming an artist of the very highest rank a dash of insanity or what the world calls insanity is indispensable.) He was a small-sized man—yet sharp observers noticed that, however crowded the stage might be in certain scenes, Booth never seem'd overtopt or hidden. He was singularly spontaneous and fluctuating; in the same part each rendering differ'd from any and all others. He had no stereotyped positions and made no arbitrary requirements on his fellow-performers.

As is well known to old play-goers, Booth's most effective part was Richard III. Either that, or Iago, or Shylock, or Pescara in "The Apostate," was sure to draw a crowded house. (Remember heavy pieces were much more in demand those days than now.) He was also unapproachably grand in Sir Giles Overreach, in "A New Way to Pay Old Debts," and the principal character in "The Iron Chest."

In any portraiture of Booth, those years, the Bowery Theatre, with its leading lights, and the lessee and manager, Thomas Hamblin, cannot be left out. It was at the Bowery I first saw Edwin Forrest (the play was John Howard Payne's "Brutus, or the Fall of Tarquin," and it affected me for weeks; or rather I might say permanently filter'd into my whole nature,) then in the zenith of his fame and ability. Sometimes (perhaps a veteran's benefit night,) the Bowery would group together five or six of the first-class actors of those days—Booth, Forrest, Cooper, Hamblin, and John R. Scott, for instance. At that time and here George Jones ("Count Joannes") was a young, handsome actor, and quite a favorite. I remember seeing him in the title rôle in "Julius Cæsar," and a capital performance it was.

To return specially to the manager. Thomas Hamblin made a first-rate foil to Booth, and was frequently cast with him. He had a large, shapely, imposing presence, and dark and flashing eyes. I remember well his rendering of the main rôle in Maturin's "Bertram, or the Castle of St. Aldobrand." But I thought Tom Hamblin's best acting was in the comparatively minor part of Faulconbridge in "King John"—he himself evidently revell'd in the part, and took away the house's applause from young Kean (the King) and Ellen Tree (Constance,) and everybody else on the stage—some time afterward at the Park. Some of the Bowery actresses were remarkably good. I remember Mrs. Pritchard in "Tour de Nesle," and Mrs. McClure in "Fatal Curiosity," and as Millwood in "George Barnell." (I wonder what

[130]

old fellow reading these lines will recall the fine comedietta of "The Youth That Never Saw a Woman," and the jolly acting in it of Mrs. Herring and old Gates.)

The Bowery, now and then, was the place, too, for spectacular pieces, such as "The Last Days of Pompeii," "The Lion-Doom'd" and the yet undying "Mazeppa." At one time "Jonathan Bradford, or the Murder at the Roadside Inn," had a long and crowded run; John Sefton and his brother William acted in it. I remember well the Frenchwoman Celeste, a splendid pantomimist, and her emotional "Wept of the Wishton-Wish." But certainly the main "reason for being" of the Bowery Theatre those years was to furnish the public with Forrest's and Booth's performances —the latter having a popularity and circles of enthusiastic admirers and critics fully equal to the former—though people were divided as always. For some reason or other, neither Forrest nor Booth would accept engagements at the more fashionable theatre, the Park. And it is a curious reminiscence, but a true one, that both these great actors and their performances were taboo'd

RIVULETS OF PROSE

by "polite society" in New York and Boston at
the time—probably as being too robustuous. But
no such scruples affected the Bowery.

Recalling from that period the occasion of
either Forrest or Booth, any good night at the
old Bowery, pack'd from ceiling to pit with its
audience mainly of alert, well dress'd, full-
blooded young and middle-aged men, the best
average of American-born mechanics—the emotional nature of the whole mass arous'd by the
power and magnetism of as mighty mimes as
ever trod the stage—the whole crowded audi-
torium, and what seeth'd in it, and flush'd from
its faces and eyes, to me as much a part of the
show as any—bursting forth in one of those long-
kept-up tempests of hand-clapping peculiar to
the Bowery—no dainty kid-glove business, but
electric force and muscle from perhaps 2000
full-sinew'd men—(the inimitable and chro-
matic tempest of one of those ovations to Edwin
Forrest, welcoming him back after an absence,
comes up to me this moment)—Such sounds and
scenes as here resumed will surely afford to many
old New Yorkers some fruitful recollections.

[132]

THE OLD BOWERY

I can yet remember (for I always scann'd an audience as rigidly as a play) the faces of the leading authors, poets, editors, of those times—Fenimore Cooper, Bryant, Paulding, Irving, Charles Bing, Watson Webb, N. P. Willis, Hoffman, Halleck, Mumford, Morris, Leggett, L. G. Clarke, R. A. Locke and others, occasionally peering from the first tier boxes; and even the great National Eminences, Presidents Adams, Jackson, Van Buren and Tyler, all made short visits there on their Eastern tours.

Awhile after 1840 the character of the Bowery as hitherto described completely changed. Cheap prices and vulgar programmes came in. People who of after years saw the pandemonium of the pit and the doings on the boards must not gauge by them the times and characters I am describing. Not but what there was more or less rankness in the crowd even then. For types of sectional New York those days—the streets East of the Bowery, that intersect Division, Grand, and up to Third Avenue—types that never found their Dickens, or Hogarth, or Balzac, and have pass'd away unportraitured—the young ship-

builders, cartmen, butchers, firemen, (the old-
time "soap-lock" or exaggerated "Mose" or
"Sikesey," of Chanfrau's plays,) they, too, were
always to be seen in these audiences, racy of the
East River and the Dry Dock. Slang, wit, occasional shirt sleeves, and a picturesque freedom
of looks and manners, with a rude good-nature
and restless movement, were generally noticeable. Yet there never were audiences that paid a
good actor or an interesting play the compliment
of more sustain'd attention or quicker rapport.
Then at times came the exceptionally decorous
and intellectual congregations I have hinted at;
for the Bowery really furnish'd plays and players you could get nowhere else. Notably, Booth
always drew the best hearers; and to a specimen
of his acting I will now attend in some detail.

I happen'd to see what has been reckon'd by
experts one of the most marvelous pieces of
histrionism ever known. It must have been about
1834 or '35. A favorite comedian and actress at
the Bowery, Thomas Flynn and his wife, were to
have a joint benefit, and, securing Booth for

THE OLD BOWERY

Richard, advertised the fact many days before-hand. The house fill'd early from top to bottom. There was some uneasiness behind the scenes, for the afternoon arrived, and Booth had not come from down in Maryland, where he lived. However, a few minutes before ringing-up time he made his appearance in lively condition.

After a one-act farce over, as contrast and prelude, the curtain rising for the tragedy, I can, from my good seat in the pit, pretty well front, see again Booth's quiet entrance from the side, as, with head bent, he slowly and in silence (amid the tempest of boisterous hand-clapping,) walks down the stage to the footlights with that peculiar and abstracted gesture, musingly kick-ing his sword, which he holds off from him by its sash. Though fifty years have pass'd since then, I can hear the clank, and feel the perfect fol-lowing hush of perhaps three thousand people waiting. (I never saw an actor who could make more of the said hush or wait, and hold the audi-ence in an indescribable, half-delicious, half-irritating suspense.) And so throughout the entire play, all parts, voice, atmosphere, magnetism, from

"Now is the winter of our discontent,"

to the closing death fight with Richmond, were of the finest and grandest. The latter character was play'd by a stalwart young fellow named Ingersoll. Indeed, all the renderings were wonderfully good. But the great spell cast upon the mass of hearers came from Booth. Especially was the dream scene very impressive. A shudder went through every nervous system in the audience; it certainly did through mine.

Without question Booth was royal heir and legitimate representative of the Garrick-Kemble-Siddons dramatic traditions; but he vitalized and gave an unnamable *race* to those traditions with his own electric personal idiosyncrasy. (As in all art-utterance it was the subtle and powerful something *special to the individual* that really conquer'd.)

To me, too, Booth stands for much else besides theatricals. I consider that my seeing the man those years glimps'd for me, beyond all else, that inner spirit and form—the unquestionable charm and vivacity, but intrinsic sophistication and artificiality—crystallizing rapidly upon the English stage and literature at and after Shakspere's time, and coming on accumulatively through the seventeenth and eighteenth centuries to the beginning, fifty or forty years ago, of those disintegrating, decomposing processes now authoritatively going on. Yes; although Booth must be class'd in that antique, almost extinct school, inflated, stagy, rendering Shakspere (perhaps inevitably, appropriately) from the growth of arbitrary and often cockney conventions, his genius was to me one of the grandest revelations of my life, a lesson of artistic expression. The words fire, energy, *abandon,* found in him unprecedented meanings. I never heard a speaker or actor who could give such a sting to hauteur or the taunt. I never heard from any other the charm of unswervingly perfect vocalization without trenching at all on mere melody, the province of music.

So much for a Thespian temple of New York fifty years since, where "sceptred tragedy went trailing by" under the gaze of the Dry Dock youth, and both players and auditors were of a character and like we shall never see again. And so much for the grandest histrion of modern times, as near as I can deliberately judge (and the phrenologists put my "caution" at 7)—grander, I believe, than Kean in the expression of electric passion, the prime eligibility of the tragic artist. For though those brilliant years had many fine and even magnificent actors, undoubtedly at Booth's death (in 1852) went the last and by far the noblest Roman of them all.

DEATH OF THOMAS CARLYLE

From Specimen Days & Collect (Philadelphia, 1882–3).

AND so the flame of the lamp, after long wasting and flickering, has gone out entirely.

As a representative author, a literary figure, no man else will bequeath to the future more significant hints of our stormy era, its fierce paradoxes, its din, and its struggling parturition periods, than Carlyle. He belongs to our own branch of the stock too; neither Latin nor Greek, but altogether Gothic. Rugged, mountainous, volcanic, he was himself more a French revolution than any of his volumes. In some respects, so far in the Nineteenth Century, the best equipt, keenest mind, even from the college point of view, of all Britain; only he had an ailing body. Dyspepsia is to be traced in every page, and now and then fills the page. One may include among the lessons of his life—even though

[139]

that life stretch'd to amazing length—how behind the tally of genius and morals stands the
stomach, and gives a sort of casting vote.

Two conflicting agonistic elements seem to
have contended in the man, sometimes pulling
him different ways like wild horses. He was a
cautious, conservative Scotchman, fully aware
what a fœtid gas-bag much of modern radicalism
is; but then his great heart demanded reform,
demanded change—often terribly at odds with
his scornful brain. No author ever put so much
wailing and despair into his books, sometimes
palpable, oftener latent. He reminds me of that
passage in Young's poems where as death presses
closer and closer for his prey, the soul rushes
hither and thither, appealing, shrieking, berating,
to escape the general doom.

Of short-comings, even positive blur-spots,
from an American point of view, he had serious
share.

Not for his merely literary merit, (though
that was great,)—not as "maker of books,"
but as launching into the self-complacent
atmosphere of our days a rasping, question-

ing, dislocating agitation and shock, is Carlyle's final value. It is time the English-speaking peoples had some true idea about the verteber of genius, namely power. As if they must always have it cut and bias'd to the fashion, like a lady's cloak! What a needed service he performs! How he shakes our comfortable reading circles with a touch of the old Hebraic anger and prophecy—indeed it is just the same. Not Isaiah himself more scornful, more threatening: "The crown of pride, the drunkards of Ephraim, shall be trodden under feet: And the glorious beauty which is on the head of the fat valley shall be a fading flower." (The word prophecy is much misused; it seems narrow'd to prediction merely. That is not the main sense of the Hebrew word translated "prophet"; it means one whose mind bubbles up and pours forth as a fountain, from inner, divine spontaneities revealing God. Prediction is a very minor part of prophecy. The great matter it to reveal and outpour the God-like suggestion pressing for birth in the soul. This is briefly the doctrine of the Friends or Quakers.)

Then the simplicity and amid ostensible frailty

[141]

the towering strength of this man—a hardy oak
knot, you could never wear out—an old farmer
dress'd in brown clothes, and not handsome—
his very foibles fascinating. Who cares that he
wrote about Dr. Francia, and "Shooting
Niagara"—and "the Nigger Question,"—and
didn't at all admire our United States? (I doubt
if he ever thought or said half as bad words
about us as we deserve.) How he splashes like
leviathan in the seas of modern literature and
politics! Doubtless, respecting the latter, one
needs first to realize, from actual observation, the
squalor, vice and doggedness ingrain'd in the
bulk-population of the British Islands, with the
red tape, the fatuity, the flunkeyism everywhere,
to understand the last meaning in his pages.
Accordingly, though he was no chartist or radical, I consider Carlyle's by far the most indig-
nant comment or protest anent the fruits of
feudalism today in Great Britain—the increasing
poverty and degradation of the homeless, land-
less twenty millions, while a few thousands, or
rather a few hundreds, possess the entire soil, the
money, and the fat berths. Trade and shipping,

[142]

and clubs and culture, and prestige, and guns, and a fine select class of gentry and aristocracy, with every modern improvement, cannot begin to salve or defend such stupendous hoggishness.

The way to test how much he has left his country were to consider, or try to consider, for a moment, the array of British thought, the resultant *ensemble* of the last fifty years, as existing to-day, *but with Carlyle left out.* It would be like an army with no artillery. The show were still a gay and rich one—Byron, Scott, Tennyson, and many more—horsemen and rapid infantry, and banners flying—but the last heavy roar so dear to the ear of the train'd soldier, and that settles fate and victory, would be lacking.

For the last three years we in America had transmitted glimpses of a thin-bodied, lonesome, wifeless, childless, very old man, lying on a sofa, kept out of bed by indomitable will, but, of late, never well enough to take the open air. I have noted this news from time to time in brief descriptions in the papers. A week ago I read such an item just before I started out for my custom-

ary evening stroll between eight and nine. In the
fine cold night, unusually clear, (Feb. 5, '81,) as
I walk'd some open grounds adjacent, the condition of Carlyle, and his approaching—perhaps
even then actual—death, filled me with thoughts
eluding statement, and curiously blending with
the scene. The planet Venus, an hour high in the
west, with all her volume and lustre recover'd,
(she has been shorn and languid for nearly a
year,) including an additional sentiment I never
noticed before—not merely voluptuous, Pa-
phian, steeping, fascinating—now with calm
commanding seriousness and hauteur—the Milo
Venus now. Upward to the zenith, Jupiter, Sat-
urn, and the moon past her quarter, trailing in
procession, with the Pleiades following, and the
constellation Taurus, and red Aldebaran. Not
a cloud in heaven. Orion strode through the
southeast, with his glittering belt—and a trifle
below hung the sun of the night, Sirius. Every
star dilated, more vitreous, nearer than usual.
Not as in some clear nights when the larger stars
entirely outshine the rest. Every little star or
cluster just as distinctly visible, and just as nigh.

DEATH OF THOMAS CARLYLE

Berenice's hair showing every gem, and new ones. To the northeast and north the Sickle, the Goat and kids, Cassiopea, Castor and Pollux, and the two Dippers. While through the whole of this silent indescribable show, inclosing and bathing my whole receptivity, ran the thought of Carlyle dying. (To soothe and spiritualize, and, as far as may be, solve the mysteries of death and genius, consider them under the stars at midnight.)

And now that he has gone hence, can it be that Thomas Carlyle, soon to chemically dissolve in ashes and by winds, remains an identity still? In ways perhaps eluding all the statements, lore and speculations of ten thousand years—eluding all possible statements to mortal sense—does he yet exist, a definite, vital being, a spirit, an individual—perhaps now wafted in space among those stellar systems, which, suggestive and limitless as they are, merely edge more limitless, far more suggestive systems? I have no doubt of it. In silence, of a fine night, such questions are answer'd to the soul, the best answers that can be given. With me, too, when depress'd by some specially sad event, or tearing problem, I wait till I go out under the stars for the last voiceless satisfaction.

Later Thoughts and Jottings

CARLYLE FROM AMERICAN POINTS OF VIEW

There is surely at present an inexplicable *rapport* (all the more piquant from its contradictoriness) between that deceas'd author and our United States of America—no matter whether it lasts or not.[1] As we Westerners assume definite shape, and result in formations and fruitage unknown before, it is curious with what a new sense our eyes turn to representa-

[1] It will be difficult for the future—judging by his books, personal dissympathies, &c.,—to account for the deep hold this author has taken on the present age, and the way he has color'd its method and thought. I am certainly at a loss to account for it all as affecting myself. But there could be no view, or even partial picture, of the middle and latter part of our Nineteenth Century, that did not markedly include Thomas Carlyle. In his case (as so many others, literary productions, works of art, personal identities, events,) there has been an impalpable something more effective than the palpable. Then I find no better text, (it is always important to have a definite, special, even oppositional, living man to start from,) for sending out certain speculations and comparisons for home use. Let us see what they amount to—those reactionary doctrines, fears, scornful analyses of democracy—even from the most erudite and sincere mind of Europe.

[146]

tive outgrowths of crises and personages in the Old World. Beyond question, since Carlyle's death, and the publication of Froude's memoirs, not only the interest in his books, but every personal bit regarding the famous Scotchman—his dyspepsia, his buffetings, his parentage, his paragon of a wife, his career in Edinburgh, in the lonesome nest on Craigenputtock moor, and then so many years in London—is probably wider and livelier to-day in this country than in his own land. Whether I succeed or no, I, too, reaching across the Atlantic and taking the man's dark fortune-telling of humanity and politics, would offset it all, (such is the fancy that comes to me,) by a far more profound horoscope-casting of those themes—G. F. Hegel's.[1]

First, about a chance, a never-fulfill'd vacuity

---

[1] Not the least mentionable part of the case, (a streak, it may be, of that humor with which history and fate love to contrast their gravity,) is that although neither of my great authorities during their lives consider'd the United States worthy of serious mention, all the principal works of both might not inappropriately be this day collected and bound up under the conspicuous title: "*Speculations for the use of North America, and Democracy there, with the relations of the same to Metaphysics, including Lessons and Warnings (encouragements too, and of the vastest, from the Old World to the New.*"

of this pale cast of thought—this British Hamlet from Cheyne row, more puzzling than the Danish one, with his contrivances for settling the broken and spavin'd joints of the world's government, especially its democratic dislocation. Carlyle's grim fate was cast to live and dwell in, and largely embody, the parturition agony and qualms of the old order, amid crowded accumulations of ghastly morbidity, giving birth to the new. But conceive of him (or his parents before him) coming to America, recuperated by the cheering realities and activity of our people and country—growing up and delving face-to-face resolutely among us here, especially at the West—inhaling and exhaling our limitless air and eligibilities—devoting his mind to the theories and developments of this Republic amid its practical facts as exemplified in Kansas, Missouri, Illinois, Tennessee, or Louisiana. I say *facts,* and face-to-face confrontings—so different from books, and all those quiddities and mere report in the libraries, upon which the man (it was wittily said of him at the age of thirty, that there was no one in Scotland who had glean'd so much and seen so little,) almost wholly fed, and which even his sturdy and vital mind but reflected at best.

Something of the sort narrowly escaped happening. In 1835, after more than a dozen years of trial and non-success, the author of "Sartor Resartus" removing to London, very poor, a confirmed hypochondriac, "Sartor" universally scoffed at, no literary prospects ahead, deliberately settled on one last casting-throw of the literary dice—resolv'd to compose and launch forth a book on the subject of the *French Revolution*—and if that won no higher guerdon or prize than hitherto, to sternly abandon the trade of author forever, and emigrate for good to America. But the venture turn'd out a lucky one, and there was no emigration.

Carlyle's work in the sphere of literature as he commenced and carried it out, is the same in one or two leading respects that Immanuel Kant's was in speculative philosophy. But the Scotchman had none of the stomachic phlegm and never perturb'd placidity of the Königsberg sage, and did not, like the latter, understand

his own limits, and stop when he got to the
end of them. He clears away jungle and poison-
vines and underbrush—at any rate hacks val-
iantly at them, smiting hip and thigh. Kant did
the like in his sphere, and it was all he profess'd
to do; his labors have left the ground fully pre-
pared ever since—and greater service was probably never perform'd by mortal man. But the
pang and hiatus of Carlyle seem to me to consist
in the evidence everywhere that amid a whirl of
fog and fury and cross purposes, he firmly believ'd he had a clue to the medication of the
world's ills, and that his bounden mission was to
exploit it.[1]

There were two anchors, or sheet-anchors, for
steadying, as a last resort, the Carlylean ship.
One will be specified presently. The other, perhaps the main, was only to be found in some
mark'd form of personal force, an extreme de-

[1] I hope I shall not myself fall into the error I charge upon him,
of prescribing a specific for indispensable evils. My utmost pretension
is probably but to offset that old claim of the exclusively curative
power of first-class individual men, as leaders and rulers, by the claims,
and general movement and result, of ideas. Something of the latter
kind seems to me the distinctive theory of America, of democracy, and
of the modern—or rather, I should say, it *is* democracy, and *is* the
modern.

gree of competent urge and will, a man or men
"born to command." Probably there ran through
every vein and current of the Scotchman's blood
something that warm'd up to this kind of trait
and character above aught else in the world, and
which makes him in my opinion the chief
celebrater and promulger of it in literature—
more than Plutarch, more than Shakspere. The
great masses of humanity stand for nothing—
at least nothing but nebulous raw material; only
the big planets and shining suns for him. To
ideas almost invariably languid or cold, a
number-one forceful personality was sure to
rouse his eulogistic passion and savage joy. In
such case, even the standard of duty hereinafter
rais'd was to be instantly lower'd and veil'd. All
that is comprehended under the terms republicanism and democracy were distasteful to him
from the first, and as he grew older they became
hateful and contemptible. For an undoubtedly
candid and penetrating faculty such as his, the
bearings he persistently ignored were marvellous.
For instance, the promise, nay certainty of the
democratic principle, to each and every State of

the current world, not so much of helping it to perfect legislators and executives, but as the only effectual method for surely, however slowly, training people on a large scale toward voluntarily ruling and managing themselves (the ultimate aim of political and all other development)—to gradually reduce the fact of *governing* to its minimum, and to subject all its staffs and their doings to the telescopes and microscopes of committees and parties—and greatest of all, to afford (not stagnation and obedient content, which went well enough with the feudalism and ecclesiasticism of the antique and medieval world, but) a vast and sane and recurrent ebb and tide action for those floods of the great deep that have henceforth palpably burst forever their old bounds—seems never to have enter'd Carlyle's thought. It was splendid how he refus'd any compromise to the last. He was curiously antique. In that harsh, picturesque, most potent voice and figure, one seems to be carried back from the present of the British islands more than two thousands years, to the range between Jerusalem and Tarsus. His fullest, best biographer justly says of him:

"He was a teacher and a prophet, in the Jewish sense of the word. The prophecies of Isaiah and Jeremiah have become a part of the permanent spiritual inheritance of mankind, because events proved that they had interpreted correctly the signs of their own times, and their prophecies were fulfill'd. Carlyle, like them, believ'd that he had a special message to deliver to the present age. Whether he was correct in that belief, and whether his message was a true message, remains to be seen. He has told us that our most cherish'd ideas of political liberty, with their kindred corollaries, are mere illusions, and that the progress which has seem'd to go along with them is a progress towards anarchy and social dissolution. If he was wrong, he had misused his powers. The principles of his teachings are false. He has offer'd himself as a guide upon a road of which he had no knowledge; and his own desire for himself would be the speediest oblivion both of his person and his works. If, on the other hand, he has been right; if, like his great predecessors, he has read truly the tendencies of this modern age of ours, and his teaching is authenticated by facts, then Carlyle, too, will take his place among the inspired seers."

To which I add an amendment that under no circumstances, and no matter how completely time and events disprove his lurid vaticinations, should the English-speaking world forget this man, nor fail to hold in honor his unsurpass'd conscience, his unique method, and his honest fame. Never were convictions more earnest and genuine. Never was there less of a flunkey or temporizer. Never had political progressivism a foe it could more heartily respect.

The second main point of Carlyle's utterance was the idea of *duty being done*. (It is simply a new codicil—if it be particularly new, which is by no means certain—on the time-honor'd bequest of dynasticism, the mould-eaten rules of legitimacy and kings.) He seems to have been impatient sometimes to madness when reminded by persons who thought at least as deeply as himself, that this formula, though precious, is rather a vague one, and that there are many other considerations to a philosophical estimate of each and every department either in general history or individual affairs.

Altogether, I don't know anything more

amazing than these persistent strides and throb-
bings so far through our Nineteenth Century of
perhaps its biggest, sharpest, and most erudite
brain, in defiance and discontent with everything; contemptuously ignoring, (either from
constitutional inaptitude, ignorance itself, or
more likely because he demanded a definite cure-
all here and now,) the only solace and solvent to
be had.

There is, apart from mere intellect, in the
make-up of every superior human identity, (in
its moral completeness, considered as *ensemble*,
not for that moral alone, but for the whole being, including physique,) a wondrous something
that realizes without argument, frequently without what is called education, (though I think
it the goal and apex of all education deserving
the name)—an intuition of the absolute balance,
in time and space, of the whole of this multifa-
rious, mad chaos of fraud, frivolity, hoggishness
—this revel of fools, and incredible make-believe
and general unsettledness, we call *the world;* a
soul-sight of that divine clue and unseen thread
which holds the whole congeries of things, all

history and time, and all events, however trivial,
however momentous, like a leash'd dog in the
hand of a hunter. Such soul-sight and root-
centre for the mind—mere optimism explains
only the surface of fringe of it—Carlyle was
mostly, perhaps entirely without. He seems instead to have been haunted in the play of his
mental action by a spectre, never entirely laid
from first to last, (Greek scholars, I believe, find
the same mocking and fantastic apparition
attending Aristophanes, his comedies,)—the
spectre of world-destruction.

How largest triumph or failure in human
life, in war or peace, may depend on some little
hidden centrality, hardly more than a drop of
blood, a pulse-beat, or a breath of air! It is
certain that all these weighty matters, democracy
in America, Carlyleism, and the temperament for
deepest political or literary exploration, turn on
a simple point in speculative philosophy.

The most profound theme that can occupy
the mind of man—the problem on whose solution science, art, the bases and pursuits of nations,
and everything else, including intelligent human

happiness, (here to-day, 1882, New York, Texas,
California, the same as all times, all lands,)
subtly and finally resting, depends for competent
outset and argument, is doubtless involved in
the query: What is the fusing explanation and
tie—what the relation between the (radical,
democratic) Me, the human identity of understanding, emotions, spirit, &c., on the one side,
of and with the (conservative) Not Me, the
whole of the material objective universe and
laws, with what is behind them in time and space,
on the other side? Immanuel Kant though he explain'd, or partially explain'd, as may be said, the
law of the human understanding, left this question an open one. Schelling's answer, or suggestion of answer, is (and very valuable and important, as far as it goes,) that the same general and
particular intelligence, passion, even the standards of right and wrong, which exist in a conscious and formulated state in man, exist in an
unconscious state, or in perceptible analogies,
throughout the entire universe of external Nature, in all its objects large or small, and all its
movements and processes—thus making the im-

palpable human mind, and concrete Nature, notwithstanding their duality and separation, con-
vertible, and in centrality and essence one. But G.
F. Hegel's fuller statement of the matter probably remains the last best word that has been said
upon it, up to date. Substantially adopting the
scheme just epitomized, he so carries it out and
fortifies it and merges everything in it, with certain serious gaps now for the first time fill'd, that
it becomes a coherent metaphysical system, and
substantial answer (as far as there can be any answer) to the foregoing question—a system
which, while I distinctly admit that the brain of
the future may add to, revise, and even entirely
reconstruct, at any rate beams forth to-day, in
its entirety, illuminating the thought of the universe, and satifying the mystery thereof to the
human mind, with a more consoling scientific as-
surance than any yet.

According to Hegel the whole earth, (an old
nucleus-thought, as in the Vedas, and no doubt
before, but never hitherto brought so absolutely
to the front, fully surcharged with modern
scientism and facts, and made the sole entrance

to each and all,) with its infinite variety, the past, the surroundings of to-day, or what may happen in the future, the contrarieties of material with spiritual, and of natural with artificial, are all, to the eye of the *ensemblist,* but necessary sides and unfoldings, different steps or links, in the endless process of Creative thought, which, amid numberless apparent failures and contradictions, is held together by central and never-broken unity—not contradictions of failures at all, but radiations of one consistent and eternal purpose; the whole mass of everything steadily, unerringly tending and flowing toward the permanent *utile* and *morale,* as rivers to oceans. As life is the whole law and incessant effort of the visible universe, and death only the other invisible side of the same, so the *utile,* so truth, so health, are the unseen but immutable laws of the moral universe, and vice and disease, with all their perturbations, are but transient, even if ever so prevalent expressions.

To politics throughout, Hegel applies the like catholic standard and faith. Not any one party, or any one form of government, is absolutely and exclusively true. Truth consists in the just relations of objects to each other. A majority or democracy may rule as outrageously and do as great harm as an oligarchy or despotism—though far less likely to do so. But the great evil is either a violation of the relations just referr'd to, or of the moral law. The specious, the unjust, the cruel, and what is called the unnatural, though not only permitted but in a certain sense, (like shade to light,) inevitable in the divine scheme, are, by the whole constitution of that scheme, partial, inconsistent, temporary, and, though having ever so great an ostensible majority, are certainly destin'd to failure, after causing great suffering.

Theology, Hegel translates into science.[1] All apparent contradictions in the statement of the Deific nature by different ages, nations, churches, points of view, are but fractional and imperfect expressions of one essential unity, from which they all proceed—crude endeavors or distorted parts, to be regarded both as distinct and united. In short (to put it in our own form, or summing

[1] I am much indebted to J. Gostick's abstract.

up,) that thinker or analyzer or overlooker who by an inscrutable combination of train'd wisdom and natural intuition most fully accepts in perfect faith the moral unity and sanity of the creative scheme, in history, science, and all life and time, present and future, is both the truest cosmical devotee or religioso, and the profoundest philosopher. While he who, by the spell of himself and his circumstance, sees darkness and despair in the sum of the workings of God's providence, and who, in that, denies or prevaricates, is, no matter how much piety plays on his lips, the most radical sinner and infidel.

I am the more assured in recounting Hegel a little freely here,[1] not only for offsetting the Carlylean letter and spirit—cutting it out all and several from the very roots, and below the roots

---

[1] I have deliberately repeated it all, not only in offset to Carlyle's everlurking pessimism and world-decadence, but as presenting the most thoroughly *American points of view* I know. In my opinion the above formulas of Hegel are an essential and crowning justification of New World democracy in the creative realms of time and space. There is that about them which only the vastness, the multiplicity and the vitality of America would seem able to comprehend, to give scope and illustration to, or to be fit for, or even originate. It is strange to me that they were born in Germany, or in the Old World at all. While a Carlyle, I should say, is quite the legitimate European product to be expected.

—but to counterpoise, since the late death and deserv'd apotheosis of Darwin, the tenets of the evolutionists. Unspeakably precious as those are to biology, and henceforth indispensable to a right aim and estimate in study, they neither comprise or explain everything—and the last word or whisper still remains to be breathed, after the utmost of those claims, floating high and forever above them all, and above technical metaphysics. While the contributions which German Kant and Fichte and Schelling and Hegel have bequeath'd to humanity—and which English Darwin has also in his field—are indispensable to the erudition of America's future, I should say that in all of them, and the best of them, when compared with the lightning flashes and flights of the old prophets and *exaltés*, the spiritual poets and poetry of all lands, (as in the Hebrew Bible,) there seems to be, nay certainly is, something lacking—something cold, a failure to satisfy the deepest emotions of the soul—a want of living glow, fondness, warmth, which the old *exaltés* and poets supply, and which the keenest modern philosophers so far do not.

DEATH OF THOMAS CARLYLE

Upon the whole, and for our purposes, this man's name certainly belongs on the list with the just-specified, first-class moral physicians of our current era—and with Emerson and two or three others—though his prescription is drastic, and perhaps destructive, while theirs is assimilating, normal and tonic. Feudal at the core, and mental offspring and radiation of feudalism as are his books, they afford ever-valuable lessons and affinities to democratic America. Nations or individuals, we surely learn deepest from unlikeness, from a sincere opponent, from the light thrown even scornfully on dangerous spots and liabilities. (Michelangelo invoked heaven's special protection against his friends and affectionate flatterers; palpable foes he could manage for himself.) In many particulars Carlyle was indeed, as Froude terms him, one of those far-off Hebraic utterers, a new Micah or Habbakuk. His words at times bubble forth with abysmic inspiration. Always precious, such men; as precious now as any time. His rude, rasping, taunting, contradictory tones—what ones are more wanted amid the supple, polish'd, money-worshipping, Jesus-and-Judas-equalizing, suffrage-sovereignty echoes of current America? He has lit up our Nineteenth Century with the light of a powerful, penetrating, and perfectly honest intellect of the first-class, turn'd on British and European politics, social life, literature, and representative personages—thoroughly dissatisfied with all, and mercilessly exposing the illness of all. But while he announces the malady, and scolds and raves about it, he himself, born and bred in the same atmosphere, is a mark'd illustration of it.

SLANG IN AMERICA

From November Boughs (Philadelphia, 1888).

VIEW'D freely, the English language is the accretion and growth of every dialect, race and range of time, and is both the free and compacted composition of all. From this point of view, it stands for Language in the largest sense, and is really the greatest of studies. It involves so much; is indeed a sort of universal absorber, combiner, and conqueror. The scope of its etymologies is the scope not only of man and civilization, but the history of Nature in all departments, and of the organic Universe, brought up to date; for all are comprehended in words, and their backgrounds. This is when words become vitaliz'd, and stand for things, as they unerringly and soon come to do, in the mind that enters on their study with fitting spirit, grasp, and appreciation.

[165]

RIVULETS OF PROSE

Slang, profoundly consider'd, is the lawless germinal element, below all words and sentences, and behind all poetry, and proves a certain perennial rankness and protestantism in speech. As the United States inherit by far their most precious possession—the language they talk and write—from the Old World, under and out of its feudal institutes, I will allow myself to borrow a simile even of those forms farthest removed from American Democracy. Considering Language then as some mighty potentate, into the majestic audience-hall of the monarch ever enters a personage like one of Shakspere's clowns, and takes position there, and plays a part even in the stateliest ceremonies. Such is Slang, or indirection, an attempt of common humanity to escape from bald literalism, and express itself illimitably, which in highest walks produces poets and poems, and doubtless in pre-historic times gave the start to, and perfected, the whole immense tangle of the old mythologies. For, curious as it may appear, it is strictly the same impulse-source, the same thing. Slang, too, is the wholesome fermentation or eructation of those processes eternally active in language, by which froth and specks are thrown up, mostly to pass away; though occasionally to settle and permanently crystallize.

To make it plainer, it is certain that many of the oldest and solidest words we use, were originally generated from the daring and license of slang. In the process of word-formation, myriads die, but here and there the attempt attracts superior meanings, becomes valuable and indispensable, and lives forever. Thus the term *right* means literally only straight. *Wrong* primarily meant twisted, distorted. *Integrity* meant oneness. *Spirit* meant breath, or flame. A *supercilious* person was one who rais'd his eyebrows. To *insult* was to leap against. If you *influenc'd* a man, you but flow'd into him. The Hebrew word which is translated *prophesy* meant to bubble up and pour forth as a fountain. The enthusiast bubbles up with the Spirit of God within him, and it pours forth from him like a fountain. The word prophecy is misunderstood. Many suppose that it is limited to mere prediction; that is but the lesser portion of prophecy. The greater

[167]

work is to reveal God. Every true religious enthusiast is a prophet.

Language, be it remember'd, is not an abstract
construction of the learn'd, or of dictionary-
makers, but is something arising out of the work,
needs, ties, joys, affections, tastes, of long generations of humanity, and has its bases broad and
low, close to the ground. Its final decisions are
made by the masses, people nearest the concrete,
having most to do with actual land and sea. It
impermeates all, the Past as well as the Present,
and is the grandest triumph of the human intellect. "Those mighty works of art," say Adding-
ton Symonds, "which we call languages, in the
construction of which whole peoples uncon-
sciously co-operated, the forms of which were
determin'd not by individual genius, but by the
instincts of successive generations, acting to one
end, inherent in the nature of the race—those
poems of pure thought and fancy, cadenced not
in words, but in living imagery, fountain-heads
of inspiration, mirrors of the mind of nascent
nations, which we call Mythologies—these surely
are more marvellous in their infantine spon-

taneity than any more mature production of the races which evolv'd them. Yet we are utterly ignorant of their embryology; the true science of Origins is yet in its cradle."

Daring as it is to say so, in the growth of Language it is certain that the retrospect of slang from the start would be the recalling from their nebulous condition of all that is poetical in the stores of human utterance. Moreover, the honest delving, as of late years, by the German and British workers in comparative philology, has pierc'd and dispers'd many of the falsest bubbles of centuries; and will disperse many more. It was long recorded that in Scandinavian mythology the heroes in the Norse Paradise drank out of the skulls of their slain enemies. Later investigation proves the word taken for skulls to mean *horns* of beasts slain in the hunt. And what reader had not been exercis'd over the traces of that feudal custom, by which *seigneurs* warm'd their feet in the bowels of serfs, the abdomen being open'd for the purpose? It now is made to appear that the serf was only required to submit his unharm'd abdomen as a foot cushion

[169]

while his lord supp'd, and was required to chafe
the legs of the seigneur with his hands.

It is curiously in embryons and childhood, and
among the illiterate, we always find the ground-
work and start of this great science, and its
noblest products. What a relief most people have
in speaking of a man not by his true formal
name, with a "Mister" to it, but by some odd
or homely appellative. The propensity to ap-
proach a meaning not directly and squarely, but
by circuitous styles of expression, seems indeed
a born quality of the common people everywhere,
evidenced by nick-names, and the inveterate determination of the masses to bestow sub-titles,
sometimes ridiculous, sometimes very apt. Always among the soldiers during the Secession
War, one heard of "Little Mac" (Gen. McClel-
lan), or of "Uncle Billy" (Gen. Sherman). "The
old man" was, of course, very common. Among
the rank and file, both armies, it was very general
to speak of the different States they came from
by their slang name. Those from Maine were
call'd Foxes; New Hampshire, Granite Boys;
Massachusetts, Bay Staters; Vermont, Green

Mountain Boys; Rhode Island, Gun Flints; Connecticut, Wooden Nutmegs; New York, Knickerbockers; New Jersey, Clam Catchers; Pennsylvania, Logher Heads; Delaware, Muskrats; Maryland, Claw Thumpers; Virginia; Beagles; North Carolina, Tar Boilers; South Carolina, Weasels; Georgia, Buzzards; Louisiana, Creoles; Alabama, Lizards; Kentucky, Corn Crackers; Ohio, Buckeyes; Michigan, Wolverines; Indiana, Hoosiers; Illinois, Suckers; Missouri, Pukes; Mississippi, Tad Poles; Florida, Fly up the Creeks; Wisconsin, Badgers; Iowa, Hawkeyes; Oregon, Hard Cases. Indeed I am not sure but slang names have more than once made Presidents. "Old Hickory" (Gen. Jackson) is one case in point. "Tippecanoe, and Tyler too," another.

I find the same rule in the people's conversations everywhere. I heard this among the men of the city horse-cars, where the conductor is often call'd a "snatcher" (i. e. because his characteristic duty is to constantly pull or snatch the bell-strap, to stop or go on.) Two young fellows are having a friendly talk, amid which, says 1st conductor, "What did you do before you was a

snatcher?" Answer of 2d conductor, "Nail'd."
(Translation of answer: "I work'd as carpen-
ter.") What is a "boom"? says one editor to another. "Esteem'd contemporary," says the other,
"a boom is a bulge." "Barefoot whiskey" is the
Tennessee name for the undiluted stimulant. In
the slang of the New York common restaurant
waiters a plate of ham and beans is known as
"stars and stripes," codfish balls as "sleeve-but-
tons," and hash as "mystery."

The Western States of the Union are however,
as may be supposed, the special areas of slang,
not only in conversation, but in names of locali-
ties, towns, rivers, etc. A late Oregon traveller
says:

"On your way to Olympia by rail, you cross a
river called the Shookum-Chuk; your train stops at
places named Newaukum, Tumwater, and Toutle;
and if you seek further you will hear of whole coun-
ties labell'd Wahkiakum, or Snohomish, or Kitsar,
or Klikatat; and Cowlitz, Hookium, and Nenolelops
greet and offend you. They complain in Olympia that
Washington Territory gets but little immigration;
but what wonder? What man, having the whole

American continent to choose from, would willingly
date his letters from the county of Snohomish or
bring up his children in the city of Nenolelops? The
village of Tumwater is, as I am ready to bear witness,
very pretty indeed; but surely an emigrant would
think twice before he establish'd himself either there
or at Toutle. Seattle is sufficiently barbarous; Steli-
coom is no better; and I suspect that the Northern
Pacific Railroad terminus has been fixed at Tacoma
because it is one of the few places on Puget Sound
whose name does not inspire horror."

Then a Nevada paper chronicles the departure
of a mining party from Reno: "The toughest
set of roosters that ever shook the dust off any
town left Reno yesterday for the new mining
district of Cornucopia. They came here from
Virginia. Among the crowd were four New
York cock-fighters, two Chicago murderers,
three Baltimore bruisers, one Philadelphia prize-
fighter, four San Francisco hoodlums, three
Virginia beats, two Union Pacific roughs, and
two check guerrillas." Among the far-west
newspapers, have been, or are, *The Fairplay*
(Colorado) *Flume, The Solid Muldoon,* of
Ouray, *The Tombstone Epitaph,* of Nevada,

The Jimplecute, of Texas, and *The Bazoo,* of Missouri. Shirttail Bend, Whiskey Flat, Puppytown, Wild Yankee Ranch, Squaw Flat, Rawhide Ranch, Loafer's Ravine, Squitch Gulch, Toenail Lake, are a few of the names of places in Butte county, Cal.

Perhaps indeed no place or term gives more luxuriant illustrations of the fermentation processes I have mention'd, and their froth and specks, than those Mississippi and Pacific coast regions, at the present day. Hasty and grotesque as are some of the names, others are of an appropriateness and originality unsurpassable. This applies to the Indian words, which are often perfect. Oklahoma is proposed in Congress for the name of one of our new Territories. Hog-eye, Lick-skillet, Rake-pocket and Steal-easy are the names of some Texan towns. Miss Bremer found among the aborigines the following names: *Men's,* Horn-point; Round-Wind; Stand-and-look-out; The-Cloud-that-goes-aside; Iron-toe; Seek-the-sun; Iron-flash; Red-bottle; White-spindle; Black-dog; Two-feathers-of-honor;

SLANG IN AMERICA

Gray-grass; Bushy-tail; Thunder-face; Go-on-the-burning-sod; Spirits-of-the-dead. *Women's,* Keep-the-fire; Spiritual-woman; Second-daughter-of-the-house; Blue-bird.

Certainly philologists have not given enough attention to this element and its results, which, I repeat, can probably be found working every where to-day, amid modern conditions, with as much life and activity as in far-back Greece or India, under prehistoric ones. Then the wit—the rich flashes of humor and genius and poetry—darting out often from a gang of laborers, railroadmen, miners, drivers or boatmen! How often have I hover'd at the edge of a crowd of them, to hear their repartees and impromptus! You get more real fun from half an hour with them than from the books of all "the American humorists."

The science of language has large and close analogies in geological science, with its ceaseless evolution, its fossils, and its numberless submerged layers and hidden strata, the infinite go-before of the present. Or, perhaps Language is

[175]

more like some vast living body, or perennial body of bodies. And slang not only brings the first feeders of it, but is afterward the start of fancy, imagination and humor, breathing into its nostrils the breath of life.

DARWINISM

From Specimen Days & Collect (Philadelphia, 1882–3).

RUNNING through prehistoric ages—coming down from them into the daybreak of our records, founding theology, suffusing literature, and so brought onward—(a sort of verteber and marrow to all the antique races and lands, Egypt, India, Greece, Rome, the Chinese, the Jews, &c., and giving cast and complexion to their art, poems, and their politics as well as ecclesiasticism, all of which we more or less inherit,) appear those venerable claims to origin from God himself, or from gods and goddesses—ancestry from divine beings of vaster beauty, size, and power than ours. But in current and latest times, the theory of human origin that seems to have most made its mark, (curiously reversing the antique,) is that we have come on, originated, developt, from monkeys, baboons—a theory

[177]

more significant perhaps in its indirections, or
what it necessitates, than it is even in itself. (Of
the twain, far apart as they seem, and angrily
as their conflicting advocates to-day oppose each
other, are not both theories to be possibly recon-
ciled, and even blended? Can we, indeed, spare
either of them? Better still, out of them is not a
third theory, the real one, or suggesting the real
one, to arise?)

Of this old theory, evolution, as broach'd
anew, trebled, with indeed all-devouring claims,
by Darwin, it has so much in it, and is so needed
as a counterpoise to yet widely prevailing and
unspeakably tenacious, enfeebling superstitions
—is fused, by the new man, into such grand,
modest, truly scientific accompaniments—that
the world of erudition, both moral and physical,
cannot but be eventually better'd and broaden'd
in its speculations, from the advent of Darwin-
ism. Nevertheless, the problem of origins, human
and other, is not the least whit nearer its solution.
In due time the Evolution theory will have to
abate its vehemence, cannot be allow'd to dominate everything else, and will have to take its

place as a segment of the circle, the cluster—as but one of many theories, many thoughts, of profoundest value—and re-adjusting and differentiating much, yet leaving the divine secrets just as inexplicable and unreachable as before—may-be more so.

Then furthermore—What is finally to be done by priest or poet—and by priest or poet only—amid all the stupendous and dazzling novelties of our century, with the advent of America, and of science and democracy—remains just as indispensable, after all the work of the ground astronomers, chemists, linguists, historians, and explorers of the last hundred years—and the wondrous German and other metaphysicians of that time—and will continue to remain, needed, America and here, just the same as in the world of Europe, or Asia, of a hundred, or a thousand, or several thousand years ago. I think indeed *more* needed, to furnish statements from the present points, the added arriere, and the unspeakably immenser vistas of to-day. Only the priests and poets of the modern, at least as exalted as any in the past, fully absorbing and ap-

[179]

preciating the results of the past, in the commonalty of all humanity, all time, (the main results already, for there is perhaps nothing more, or at any rate not much, strictly new, only more important modern combinations, and new relative adjustments,) must indeed recast the old metal, the already achiev'd material, into and through new moulds, current forms.

Meantime, the highest and subtlest and broadest truths of modern science wait for their true assignment and last vivid flashes of light—as Democracy waits for its—through first-class metaphysicians and speculative philosophs—laying the basements and foundations for those new, more expanded, more harmonious, more melodious, freer American poems.

EMERSON'S BOOKS (THE SHADOWS OF THEM)

From Specimen Days & Collect (Philadelphia, 1882–3).

IN the regions we call Nature, towering beyond all measurement with infinite spread, infinite depth and height—in those regions, including Man, socially and historically, with his moral-emotional influences—how small a part, (it came in my mind to-day,) has literature really depicted—even summing up all of it, all ages. Seems at its best some little fleet of boats, hugging the shores of a boundless sea, and never venturing, exploring the unmapp'd—never, Columbus-like, sailing out for New Worlds, and to complete the orb's rondure. Emerson writes frequently in the atmosphere of this thought, and his books report one or two things from that very ocean and air, and more legibly address'd to our age and American polity than by any man yet. But

[181]

I will begin by scarifying him—thus proving that I am not insensible to his deepest lessons. I will consider his books from a democratic and western point of view. I will specify the shadows on these sunny expanses. Somebody has said of heroic character that "wherever the tallest peaks are present, must inevitably be deep chasms and valleys." Mine be the ungracious task (for reasons) of leaving unmention'd both sunny expanses and sky-reaching heights, to dwell on the bare spots and darknesses. I have a theory that no artist or work of the very first class may be or can be without them.

First, then, these pages are perhaps too perfect, too concentrated. (How good, for instance, is good butter, good sugar. But to be eating nothing but sugar and butter all the time! even if ever so good.) And though the author has much to say of freedom and wildness and simplicity and spontaneity, no performance was ever more based on artificial scholarships and decorums at third or fourth removes, (he calls it culture,) and built up from them. It is always a *make*, never an unconscious *growth*. It is the porcelain

figure or statuette of lion, or stag, or Indian
hunter—and a very choice statuette too—appropriate for the rosewood or marble bracket of
parlor or library; never the animal itself, or the
hunter himself. Indeed, who wants the real
animal or hunter? What would that do amid
astral and bric-a-brac and tapestry, and ladies
and gentlemen talking in subdued tones of
Browning and Longfellow and art? The least
suspicion of such actual bull, or Indian, or of
Nature carrying out itself, would put all those
good people to instant terror and flight.

Emerson, in my opinion, is not most eminent
as a poet or artist or teacher, though valuable
in all those. He is best as critic, or diagnoser. Not
passion or imagination or warp or weakness, or
any pronounced cause or specialty, dominates
him. Cold and bloodless intellectuality dominates
him. (I know the fires, emotions, love, egotisms,
glow deep, perennial, as in all New Englanders
—but the façade hides them well—they give
no sign.) He does not see or take one side, one
presentation only or mainly, (as all the poets, or
most of the fine writers anyhow)—he sees all

sides. His final influence is to make his students cease to worship anything—almost cease to believe in anything, outside of themselves. These books will fill, and well fill, certain stretches of life, certain stages of development—are, (like the tenets or theology the author of them preach'd when a young man,) unspeakably serviceable and precious as a stage. But in old or nervous or solemnest or dying hours, when one needs the impalpably soothing and vitalizing influences of abysmic Nature, or its affinities in literature or human society, and the soul resents the keenest mere intellection, they will not be sought for.

For a philosopher, Emerson possesses a singularly dandified theory of manners. He seems to have no notion at all that manners are simply the signs by which the chemist or metallurgist knows his metals. To the profound scientist, all metals are profound, as they really are. The little one, like the conventional world, will make much of gold and silver only. Then to the real artist in humanity, what are called bad manners are often the most picturesque and significant of

[184]

all. Suppose these books becoming absorb'd, the permanent chyle of American general and particular character—what a well-wash'd and grammatical, but bloodless and helpless, race we should turn out! No, no, dear friend; though the States want scholars, undoubtedly, and perhaps want ladies and gentlemen who use the bath frequently, and never laugh loud, or talk wrong, they don't want scholars, or ladies and gentlemen, at the expense of all the rest. They want good farmers, sailors, mechanics, clerks, citizens —perfect business and social relations—perfect fathers and mothers. If we could only have these, or their approximations, plenty of them, fine and large and sane and generous and patriotic, they might make their verbs disagree from their nominatives, and laugh like volleys of musketeers, if they should please. Of course these are not all America wants, but they are first of all to be provided on a large scale. And, with tremendous errors and escapades, this, substantially, is what the States seem to have an intuition of, and to be mainly aiming at. The plan of a select class, superfined, (demarcated from the rest,)

the plan of Old World lands and literatures, is
not so objectionable in itself, but because it
chokes the true plan for us, and indeed is death
to it. As to such special class, the United States
can never produce any equal to the splendid
show, (far, far beyond comparison or competition here,) of the principal European nations,
both in the past and at the present day. But an
immense and distinctive commonalty over our
vast and varied area, west and east, south and
north—in fact, for the first time in history, a
great, aggregated, real PEOPLE, worthy the
name, and made of develop'd heroic individuals,
both sexes—is America's principal, perhaps only,
reason for being. If ever accomplish'd, it will
be at least as much, (I lately think, doubly as
much,) the result of fitting and democratic
sociologies, literatures and arts—if we ever get
them—as of our democratic politics.

At times it has been doubtful to me if Emerson
really knows or feels what Poetry is at its highest,
as in the Bible, for instance, or Homer or Shakspere. I see he covertly or plainly likes best superb
verbal polish, or something old or odd—Waller's

EMERSON'S BOOKS (SHADOWS OF THEM)

"Go, lovely rose," or Lovelace's lines "to Lucusta"
—the quaint conceits of the old French bards,
and the like. Of *power* he seems to have a gentleman's admiration—but in his inmost heart the
grandest attribute of God and Poets is always
subordinate to the octaves, conceits, polite kinks,
and verbs.

The reminiscence that years ago I began like
most youngsters to have a touch (though it came
late, and was only on the surface) of Emerson-
on-the-brain—that I read his writings reverently,
and address'd him in print as "Master," and for
a month or so thought of him as such—I retain
not only with composure, but positive satisfaction. I have noticed that most young people of
eager minds pass through this stage of exercise.

The best part of Emersonianism is, it breeds
the giant that destroys itself. Who wants to be
any man's mere follower? lurks behind every
page. No teacher ever taught, that has so provided for his pupil's setting up independently—
no truer evolutionist.

[187]

POETRY OF THE FUTURE

From The North American Review, February, 1881.

STRANGE as it may seem, the topmost proof of a race is its own born poetry. The presence of that, or the absence, each tells its story. As the flowering rose or lily, as the ripen'd fruit to a tree, the apple or the peach, no matter how fine the trunk, or copious or rich the branches and foliage, here waits *sine qua non* at last. The stamp of entire and finish'd greatness to any nation, to the American Republic among the rest, must be sternly withheld till it has put what it stands for in the blossom of original, first-class poems. No imitations will do.

And though no *esthetik* worthy the present condition or future certainties of the New World seems to have been outlined in men's mind, or has been generally called for, or thought needed, I am clear that until the United States have just such definite and native expressers in the highest

[188]

artistic fields, their mere political, geographical, wealth-forming, and even intellectual eminence, however astonishing and predominate, will constitute but a more and more expanded and well-appointed body, and perhaps brain, with little or no soul. Sugar-coat the grim truth as we may, and ward off with outward plausible words, denials, explanations, to the mental inward perception of the land this blank is plain; a barren void exists. For the meanings and maturer purposes of these States are not the constructing of a new world of politics merely, and physical comforts for the million, but even more determinedly, in range with science and the modern, of a new world of democratic sociology and imaginative literature. If the latter were not establish'd for the States, to form their only permanent tie and hold, the first-named would be of little avail.

With the poems of a first-class land are twined, as weft with warp, its types of personal character, of individuality, peculiar, native, its own physiognomy, man's and woman's, its own shapes, forms, and manners, fully justified under the eternal laws of all forms, all manners, all

times. The hour has come for democracy in
America to inaugurate itself in the two direc-
tions specified—autochthonic poems and personalities—born expressers of itself, its spirit
alone, to radiate in subtle ways, not only in art,
but the practical and familiar, in the transactions between employers and employ'd persons,
in business and wages, and sternly in the army
and navy, and revolutionizing them. I find nowhere a scope profound enough, and radical and
objective enough, either for aggregates or individuals. The thought and identity of a poetry in
America to fill, and worthily fill, the great void,
and enhance these aims, electrifying all and several, involves the essence and integral facts, real
and spiritual, of the whole land, the whole body.
What the great sympathetic is to the congeries
of bones, joints, heart, fluids, nervous system
and vitality, constituting, launching forth in
time and space a human being—aye, an immor-
tal soul—such relation, and no less, holds true
poetry to the single personality, or to the nation.

Here our thirty-eight States stand to-day, the

children of past precedents, and, young as they are, heirs of a very old estate. One or two points we will consider, out of the myriads presenting themselves. The feudalism of the British Islands, illustrated by Shakspere—and by his legitimate followers, Walter Scott and Alfred Tennyson —with all its tyrannies, superstitions, evils, had most superb and heroic permeating veins, poems, manners; even its errors fascinating. It almost seems as if only that feudalism in Europe, like slavery in our own South, could outcrop types of tallest, noblest personal character yet— strength and devotion and love better than else- where—invincible courage, generosity, aspira- tion, the spines of all. Here is where Shakspere and the others I have named perform a service incalculably precious to our America. Politics, literature, and everything else, centers at last in perfect *personnel,* (as democracy is to find the same as the rest;) and here feudalism is unrival'd —here the rich and highest-rising lessons it be- queaths us—a mass of foreign nutriment, which we are to work over, and popularize and enlarge, and present again in our own growths.

Still there are pretty grave and anxious draw-
backs, jeopardies, fears. Let us give some reflec-
tions on the subject, a little fluctuating, but
starting from one central thought, and returning
there again. Two or three curious results may
plow up. As in the astronomical laws, the very
power that would seem most deadly and destructive turns out to be latently conservative of
longest, vastest future births and lives. We will
for once briefly examine the just-named authors
solely from a Western point of view. It may be,
indeed, that we shall use the sun of English
literature, and the brightest current stars of his
system, mainly as pegs to hang some cogitations
on, for home inspection.

As depicter and dramatist of the passions at
their stormiest outstretch, though ranking high,
Shakspere (spanning the arch wide enough) is
equal'd by several, and excell'd by the best old
Greeks, (as Æschylus). But in portraying
mediæval European lords and barons, the arrogant port, so dear to the inmost human heart,
(pride! pride! dearest, perhaps, of all—touching

us, too, of the States closest of all—closer than love,) he stands alone, and I do not wonder he so witches the world.

From first to last, also, Walter Scott and Tennyson, like Shakspere, exhale that principle of caste which we Americans have come on earth to destroy. Jefferson's verdict on the Waverley novels was that they turn'd and condens'd brilliant but entirely false lights and glamours over the lords, ladies, and aristocratic institutes of Europe, with all their measureless infamies, and then left the bulk of the suffering, downtrodden people contemptuously in the shade. Without stopping to answer this hornet-stinging criticism, or to repay any part of the debt of thanks I owe, in common with every American, to the noblest, healthiest, cheeriest romances that ever lived, I pass on to Tennyson, his works.

Poetry here of a very high (perhaps the highest) order of verbal melody, exquisitely clean and pure, and almost always perfumed, like the tuberose, to an extreme of sweetness—sometimes not, however, but even then a camellia of the hot-house, never a common flower—the verse

of inside elegance and high-life; and yet preserv-
ing amid all its super-delicatesse a smack of outdoors and outdoor folk. The old Norman lord-
hood quality here, too, cross'd with that Saxon
fiber from which twain the best current stock
of England springs—poetry that revels above
all things in traditions of knights and chivalry,
and deeds of derring-do. The odor of English
social life in its highest range—a melancholy,
affectionate, very manly, but dainty breed—
pervading the pages like an invisible scent; the
idleness, the traditions, the mannerisms, the
stately *ennui;* the yearning of love, like a spinal
marrow, inside of all; the costumes, brocade and
satin; the old houses and furniture—solid oak, no
mere veneering—the moldy secrets everywhere;
the verdure, the ivy on the walls, the moat, the
English landscape outside, the buzzing fly in the
sun inside the window pane. Never one democratic page; nay, not a line, not a word; never
free and *naïve* poetry, but involv'd, labor'd,
quite sophisticated—even when the theme is ever
so simple or rustic, (a shell, a bit of sedge, the
commonest love-passage between a lad and lass,)

the handling of the rhyme all showing the scholar
and conventional gentleman; showing the laureate, too, the *attaché* of the throne, and most
excellent, too; nothing better through the volumes than the dedication "to the Queen" at the
beginning, and the other fine dedication, "these
to his memory" (Prince Albert's,) preceding
"Idylls of the King."

Such for an off-hand summary of the mighty
three that now, by the women, men, and young
folk of the fifty millions given these States by
their late census, have been and are more read
than all others put together.

We hear it said, both of Tennyson and another current leading literary illustrator of
Great Britain, Carlyle—as of Victor Hugo in
France—that not one of them is personally
friendly or admirant toward America; indeed,
quite the reverse. *N'importe.* That they (and
more good minds than theirs) cannot span the
vast revolutionary arch thrown by the United
States over the centuries, fix'd in the present,
launch'd to the endless future; that they cannot

stomach the high-life-below-stairs coloring all our poetic and genteel social status so far—the measureless viciousness of the great radical Republic, with its ruffianly nominations and elections; its loud, ill-pitch'd voice, utterly regardless whether the verb agrees with the nominative; its fights, errors, eructations, repulsions, dishonesties, audacities; those fearful and varied and long-continued storm and stress stages (so offensive to the well-regulated college-bred mind) wherewith Nature, history, and time block out nationalities more powerful than the past, and to upturn it and press on to the future;—that they cannot understand and fathom all this, I say, is it to be wonder'd at? Fortunately, the gestation of our thirty-eight empires (and plenty more to come) proceeds on its course, on scales of area and velocity immense and absolute as the globe, and, like the globe itself, quite oblivious even of great poets and thinkers. But we can by no means afford to be oblivious of them.

The same of feudalism, its castles, courts, etiquettes, personalities. However they, or the spirits of them hovering in the air, might scowl and glower at such removes as current Kansas or Kentucky life and forms, the latter may by no means repudiate or leave out the former. Allowing all the evil that it did, we get, here and to-day, a balance of good out of its reminiscence almost beyond price.

Am I content, then, that the general interior chyle of our republic should be supplied and nourish'd by wholesale from foreign and antagonistic sources such as these? Let me answer that question briefly:

Years ago I thought Americans ought to strike out separate, and have expressions of their own in highest literature. I think so still, and more decidedly than ever. But those convictions are now strongly temper'd by some additional points, (perhaps the results of advancing age, or the reflections of invalidism.) I see that this world of the West, as part of all, fuses inseparably with the East, and with all, as time does—the ever new, yet old, old human race—"the same subject continued," as the novels of our grandfathers had it for chapter-heads. If we are not to hospitably receive and complete the inaugurations of the old civilizations, and change their small scale to the largest, broadest scale, what on earth are we for?

The currents of practical business in America, the rude, coarse, tussling facts of our lives, and all their daily experiences, need just the precipitation and tincture of this entirely different fancy world of lulling, contrasting, even feudalistic, anti-republican poetry and romance. On the enormous outgrowth of our unloos'd individualities, and the rank self-assertion of humanity here, may well fall these grace-persuading, *recherché* influences. We first require that individuals and communities shall be free; then surely comes a time when it is requisite that they shall not be too free. Although to such results in the future I look mainly for a great poetry native to us, these importations till then will have to be accepted, such as they are, and thankful they are no worse. The inmost spiritual currents of the present time curiously revenge and check their own compell'd tendency to democracy, and absorption in it, by mark'd lean-ings to the past—by reminiscences in poems, plots, operas, novels, to a far-off, contrary, deceased world, as if they dreaded the great vulgar gulf tides of to-day. Then what has been fifty centuries growing, working in, and accepted as crowns and apices for our kind, is not going to be pulled down and discarded in a hurry.

It is, perhaps, time we paid our respects directly to the honorable party, the real object of these preambles. But we must make *reconnaissance* a little further still. Not the least part of our lesson were to realize the curiosity and interest of friendly foreign experts,[1] and how our situation looks to them. "American poetry," says the London "Times,"[2] "is the poetry of apt pupils, but it is afflicted from first to last with

[1] A few years ago I saw the question, "Has America produced any great poem?" announced as prize-subject for the competition of some university in Northern Europe. I saw the item in a foreign paper and made a note of it; but being taken down with paralysis, and prostrated for a long season, the matter slipp'd away, and I have never been able since to get hold of any essay presented for the prize, or report of the discussion, nor to learn for certain whether there was any essay or discussion, nor can I now remember the place. It may have been Upsala, or possibly Heidelberg. Perhaps some German or Scandinavian can give particulars. I think it was in 1872.

[2] In a long and prominent editorial, at the time, on the death of William Cullen Bryant.

a fatal want of raciness. Bryant has been long passed as a poet by Professor Longfellow; but in Longfellow, with all his scholarly grace and tender feeling, the defect is more apparent than it was in Bryant. Mr. Lowell can overflow with American humor when politics inspire his muse; but in the realm of pure poetry he is no more American than a Newdigate prize-man. Joaquin Miller's verse has fluency and movement and harmony, but as for the thought, his songs of the sierras might as well have been written in Holland."

Unless in a certain very slight contingency, the "Times" says: "American verse, from its earliest to its latest stages, seems an exotic, with an exuberance of gorgeous blossoms, but no principle of reproduction. That is the very note and test of its inherent want. Great poets are tortured and massacred by having their flowers of fancy gathered and gummed down in the *hortus siccus* of an anthology. American poets show better in an anthology than in the collected volumes of their works. Like their audience they have been unable to resist the attraction of the vast orbit of English literature. They may talk of the primeval forest, but it would generally be very hard from internal evidence to detect that they were writing on the banks of the Hudson rather than on those of the Thames. . . . In fact, they have caught the English tone and air and mood only too faithfully, and are accepted by the superficially cultivated English intelligence as readily as if they were English born. Americans themselves confess to a certain disappointment that a literary curiosity and intelligence so diffused [as in the United States] have not taken up English literature at the point at which America has received it, and carried it forward and developed it with an independent energy. But like reader like poet. Both show the effects of having come into an estate they have not earned. A nation of readers has required of its poets a diction and symmetry of form equal to that of an old literature like that of Great Britain, which is also theirs. No ruggedness, however racy, would be tolerated by circles which, however superficial their culture, read Byron and Tennyson."

RIVULETS OF PROSE

The English critic, though a gentleman and a scholar, and friendly withal, is evidently not altogether satisfied, (perhaps he is jealous,) and winds up by saying: "For the English language to have been enriched with a national poetry which was not English but American, would have been a treasure beyond price." With which, as whet and foil, we shall proceed to ventilate more definitely certain no doubt willful opinions.

Leaving unnoticed at present the great masterpieces of the antique, or anything from the middle ages, the prevailing flow of poetry for the last fifty or eighty years, and now at its height, has been and is (like the music) an expression of mere surface melody, within narrow limits, and yet, to give it its due, perfectly satisfying to the demands of the ear, of wondrous charm, of smooth and easy delivery, and the triumph of technical art. Above all things it is fractional and select. It shrinks with aversion from the sturdy, the universal, and the democratic.

The poetry of the future, (a phrase open to

sharp criticism, and not satisfactory to me, but significant, and I will use it)—the poetry of the future aims at the free expression of emotion, (which means far, far more than appears at first,) and to arouse and initiate, more than to define or finish. Like all modern tendencies, it has direct or indirect reference continually to the reader, to you or me, to the central identity of everything, the mighty Ego. (Byron's was a vehement dash, with plenty of impatient democracy, but lurid and introverted amid all its magnetism; not at all the fitting, lasting song of a grand, secure, free, sunny race.) It is more akin, likewise, to outside life and landscape, (returning mainly to the antique feeling,) real sun and gale, and woods and shores—to the elements themselves—not sitting at ease in parlor or library listening to a good tale of them, told in good rhyme. Character, a feature far above style or polish—a feature not absent at any time, but now first brought to the fore—gives predominant stamp to advancing poetry. Its born sister, music, already responds to the same influences. "The music of the present, Wagner's, Gounod's, even

the later Verdi's, all tends toward this free expression of poetic emotion, and demands a vocal-
ism totally unlike that required for Rossini's
splendid roulades, or Bellini's suave melodies."

Is there not even now, indeed, an evolution,
a departure from the masters? Venerable and unsurpassable after their kind as are the old works,
and always unspeakably precious as studies, (for
Americans more than any other people,) is it
too much to say that by the shifted combinations
of the modern mind the whole underlying theory
of first-class verse has changed? "Formerly, during the period term'd classic," says Sainte-Beuve,
"when literature was govern'd by recognized
rules, he was consider'd the best poet who had
composed the most perfect work, the most beautiful poem, the most intelligible, the most agreeable to read, the most complete in every respect,
—the Æneid, the Gerusalemme, a fine tragedy.
To-day, something else is wanted. For us the
greatest poet is he who in his works most stimu-
lates the reader's imagination and reflection, who
excites him the most himself to poetize. The
greatest poet is not he who has done the best; it

is he who suggests the most; he, not all of whose meaning is at first obvious, and who leaves you much to desire, to explain, to study, much to complete in your turn."

The fatal defects our American singers labor under are subordination of spirit, an absence of the concrete and of real patriotism, and in excess that modern æsthetic contagion a queer friend of mine calls the *beauty disease*. "The immoderate taste for beauty and art," says Charles Baudelaire, "leads men into monstrous excesses. In minds imbued with a frantic greed for the beautiful, all the balances of truth and justice disappear. There is a lust, a disease of the art faculties, which eats up the moral like a cancer."

Of course, by our plentiful verse-writers there is plenty of service perform'd, of a kind. Nor need we go far for a tally. We see, in every polite circle, a class of accomplish'd, good-natured persons, ("society," in fact, could not get on without them,) fully eligible for certain problems, times, and duties—to mix eggnog, to mend the broken spectacles, to decide whether the stew'd eels shall precede the sherry or the sherry

the stew'd eels, to eke out Mrs. A. B.'s parlor-
tableaux with monk, Jew, lover, Puck, Prospero,
Caliban, or what not, and to generally contribute
and gracefully adapt their flexibilities and talents,
in those ranges, to the world's· service. But for
real crises, great needs and pulls, moral or
physical, they might as well have never been
born.

Or the accepted notion of a poet would appear
to be a sort of male odalisque, singing or piano-
playing a kind of spiced ideas, second-hand reminiscences, or toying late hours at entertain-
ments, in rooms stifling with fashionable scent.
I think I haven't seen a new-publish'd, healthy,
bracing, simple lyric in ten years. Not long ago,
there were verses in each of three fresh month-
lies, from leading authors, and in every one the
whole central *motif* (perfectly serious) was the
melancholiness of a marriageable young woman
who didn't get a rich husband, but a poor one!

Besides its tonic and *al fresco* physiology, re-
lieving such as this, the poetry of the future will
take on character in a more important respect.

POETRY OF THE FUTURE

Science, having extirpated the old stockfables and superstitions, is clearing a field for verse, for all the arts, and even for romance, a hundred-fold ampler and more wonderful, with the new principles behind. Republicanism advances over the whole world. Liberty, with Law by her side, will one day be paramount—will at any rate be the central idea. Then only—for all the splendor and beauty of what has been, or the polish of what is—then only will the true poets appear, and the true poems. Not the satin and patchouly of today, not the glorification of the butcheries and wars of the past, nor any fight between Deity on one side and somebody else on the other—not Milton, not even Shakspere's plays, grand as they are. Entirely different and hitherto unknown classes of men, being authoritatively called for in imaginative literature, will certainly appear. What is hitherto most lacking, perhaps most absolutely indicates the future. Democracy has been hurried on through time by measureless tides and winds, resistless as the revolution of the globe, and as far-reaching and rapid. But in the highest walks of art it has not yet had a single representative worthy of it anywhere upon the earth.

Never had real bard a task more fit for sublime ardor and genius than to sing worthily the songs these States have already indicated. Their origin, Washington, '76, the picturesqueness of old times, the War of 1812 and the seafights; the incredible rapidity of movement and breadth of area—to fuse and compact the South and North, the East and West, to express the native forms, situations, scenes, from Montauk to California, and from the Saguenay to the Rio Grande—the working out on such gigantic scales, and with such a swift and mighty play of changing light and shade, of the great problems of man and freedom,—how far ahead of the stereotyped plots, or gem-cutting, or tales of love, or wars of mere ambition! Our history is so full of spinal, modern, germinal subjects—one above all. What the ancient siege of Ilium, and the puissance of Hector's and Agamemnon's warriors proved to Hellenic art and literature, and all art and literature since, may prove the war of attempted secession of 1861–'65 to the future æsthetics, drama, romance, poems of the United States.

Nor could utility itself provide anything more practically serviceable to the hundred millions who, a couple of generations hence, will inhabit within the limits just named, than the permeation of a sane, sweet, autochthonous national poetry—must I say of a kind that does not now exist? but which, I fully believe, will in time be supplied on scales as free as Nature's elements. (It is acknowledged that we of the States are the most materialistic and money-making people ever known. My own theory, while fully accepting this, is that we are the most emotional, spiritualistic, and poetry-loving people also.)

Infinite are the new and orbic traits waiting to be launch'd forth in the firmament that is, and is to be, America. Lately, I have wonder'd whether the last meaning of this cluster of thirty-eight States is not only practical fraternity among themselves—the only real *union*, (much nearer its accomplishment, too, than appears on the surface)—but for fraternity over the whole globe—that dazzling, pensive dream of ages! Indeed, the peculiar glory of our lands, I have come to see, or expect to see, not in their geographical or republican greatness, nor wealth or products, nor military or naval power, nor special, eminent names in any department, to shine with, or outshine, foreign special names in similar departments,—but more and more in a vaster, saner, more surrounding Comradeship, uniting closer and closer not only the American States, but all nations, and all humanity. That, O poets! is not that a theme worth chanting, striving for? Why not fix your verses henceforth to the gauge of the round globe? the whole race? Perhaps the most illustrious culmination of the modern may thus prove to be a signal growth of joyous, more exalted bards of adhesiveness, identically one in soul, but contributed by every nation, each after its distinctive kind. Let us, audacious, start it. Let the diplomats, as ever, still deeply plan, seeking advantages, proposing treaties between governments, and to bind them, on paper: what I seek is different, simpler. I would inaugurate from America, for this purpose, new formulas—international poems. I have thought that the invisible root out of which the poetry deepest in, and dearest to, humanity grows, is Friendship. I have thought that both in patriotism and song (even amid their grandest shows past) we have adhered too long to petty limits, and that the time has come to enfold the world.

Not only is the human and artificial world we have establish'd in the West a radical departure from anything hitherto known—not only men and politics, and all that goes with them —but Nature itself, in the main sense, its construction, is different. The same old font of type, of course, but set up to a text never composed or issued before. For Nature consists not only in itself, objectively, but at least just as much in its subjective reflection from the person, spirit, age, looking at it, in the midst of it, and absorbing it—faithfully sends back the characteristic beliefs of the time or individual—takes, and readily gives again, the physiognomy of any nation or literature—falls like a great elastic veil on a face, or like the molding plaster on a statue.

What is Nature? What were the elements, the invisible backgrounds and eidólons of it, to Homer's heroes, voyagers, gods? What all through the wanderings of Virgil's Æneas? Then to Shakspere's characters—Hamlet, Lear, the English-Norman kings, the Romans? What was Nature to Rousseau, to Voltaire, to the German Goethe in his little classical court gardens? In those presentments in Tennyson (see the "Idyls of the King"—what sumptuous, perfumed, arras-and-gold Nature, inimitably described, better than any, fit for princes and knights and peerless ladies—wrathful or peaceful, just the same—Vivien and Merlin in their strange dalliance, or the death-float of Elaine, or Geraint and the long journey of his disgraced Enid and himself through the wood, and the wife all day driving the horses,) as in all the great imported art-works, treatises, systems, from Lucretius down, there is a constantly lurking, often pervading something, that will have to be eliminated, as not only unsuited to modern democracy and science in America, but insulting to them, and disproved by them.[1]

Still, the rule and demesne of poetry will always be not the exterior, but interior; not the macrocosm, but microcosm; not Nature, but Man. I haven't said anything about the imperative need of a race of giant bards in the future, to hold up high to eyes of land and race the eternal antiseptic models, and to dauntlessly confront greed, injustice, and all forms of that wiliness and tyranny whose roots never die— (my opinion is, that after all the rest is advanced, *that* is what first-class poets are for; as, to their days and occasions, the Hebrew lyrists, Roman Juvenal, and doubtless the old singers of India, and the British Druids)—to counteract dangers, immensest ones, already looming in America— measureless corruption in politics—what we call religion, a mere mask of wax or lace;—for *ensemble*, that most cankerous, offensive of all earth's shows—a vast and varied community,

---

[1] Whatever may be said of the few principal poems—or their best passages—it is certain that the overwhelming mass of poetic works, as now absorb'd into human character, exerts a certain constipating, repressing, in-door, and artificial influence, impossible to elude—seldom or never that freeing, dilating, joyous one, with which uncramp'd Nature works on every individual without exception.

prosperous and fat with wealth of money and products and business ventures—plenty of mere intellectuality too—and then utterly without the sound, prevailing, moral and æsthetic health-action beyond all the money and mere intellect of the world.

Is it a dream of mine that, in times to come, west, south, east, north, will silently, surely arise a race of such poets, varied, yet one in soul— nor only poets, and of the best, but newer, larger prophets—larger than Judea's, and more passionate—to meet and penetrate those woes, as shafts of light the darkness?

As I write, the last fifth of the Nineteenth Century is enter'd upon, and will soon be waning. Now, and for a long time to come, what the United States most need, to give purport, definiteness, reason why, to their unprecedented material wealth, industrial products, education by rote merely, great populousness and intellectual activity, is the central, spinal reality, (or even the idea of it,) of such a democratic band of native-born-and-bred teachers, artists, *littéra-*

teurs, tolerant and receptive of importations, but entirely adjusted to the West, to ourselves, to our own days, combinations, differences, superiorities. Indeed, I am fond of thinking that the whole series of concrete and political triumphs of the Republic are mainly as bases and preparations for half a dozen future poets, ideal personalities, referring not to a special class, but to the entire people, four or five millions of square miles.

Long, long are the processes of the development of a nationality. Only to the rapt vision does the seen become the prophecy of the unseen.[1] Democracy, so far attending only to the

[1] Is there not such a thing as the philosophy of American history and politics? And if so, what is it? . . . Wise men say there are two sets of wills to nations and to persons—one set that acts and works from explainable motives—from teaching, intelligence, judgment, circumstance, caprice, emulation, greed, &c.—and then another set, perhaps deep, hidden, unsuspected, yet often more potent than the first, refusing to be argued with, rising as it were out of abysses, resistlessly urging on speakers, doers, communities, unwitting to themselves—the poet to his fieriest words—the race to pursue its loftiest ideal. Indeed, the paradox of a nation's life and career, with all its wondrous contradictions, can probably only be explain'd from these two wills, sometimes conflicting, each operating in its sphere, combining in races or in persons, and producing strangest results.

Let us hope there is (indeed, can there be any doubt there is?) this great unconscious and abysmic second will also running through the average nationality and career of America. Let us hope that, amid all the dangers and defections of the present, and through all the

RIVULETS OF PROSE

real, is not for the real only, but the grandest
ideal to justify the modern by that, and not only
to equal, but to become by that superior to the
past. On a comprehensive summing up of the

processes of the conscious will, it alone is the permanent and sovereign
force, destined to carry on the New World to fulfill its destinies in
the future—to resolutely pursue those destinies, are upon age; to
build, far, far beyond its past vision, present thought; to form and
fashion, and for the general type, men and women more noble, more
athletic than the world has yet seen; to gradually, firmly blend, from
all the States, with all varieties, a friendly, happy, free, religious
nationality—a nationality not only the richest, most inventive, most
productive and materialistic the world has yet known, but compacted
indissolubly, and out of whose ample and solid bulk, and giving purpose and finish to it, conscience, morals, and all the spiritual attributes,
shall surely rise, like spires above some group of edifices, firm-footed
on the earth, yet scaling space and heaven.

Great as they are, and greater far to be, the United States, too,
are but a series of steps in the eternal process of creative thought.
And here is, to my mind, their final justification, and certain perpetuity.
There is in that sublime process, in the laws of the universe—and,
above all, in the moral law—something that would make unsatisfac-
tory, and, even vain and contemptible, all the triumphs of war, the
gains of peace, and the proudest worldly grandeur of all the nations
that have ever existed, or that (ours included) now exist, except that
we constantly see, through all their worldly career, however struggling
and blind and lame, attempts, by all ages, all peoples, according to
their development, to reach, to press, to progress on, and ever farther
on, to more and more advanced ideals.

The glory of the republic of the United States, in my opinion, is
to be that, emerging in the light of the modern and the splendor
of science, and solidly based on the past, it is to cheerfully range itself,
and its politics are henceforth to come, under those universal laws,
and embody them, and carry them out, to serve them. And as only that
individual becomes truly great who understands well that, while complete in himself in a certain sense, he is but a part of the divine, eternal
scheme, and whose special life and laws are adjusted to move in harmonious relations with the general laws of Nature, and especially with
the moral law, the deepest and highest of all, and the last vitality of
man or state—so the United States may only become the greatest and

[216]

POETRY OF THE FUTURE

processes and present and hitherto condition of the United States, with reference to their future, and the indispensable precedents to it, my point, below all surfaces, and subsoiling them, is, that the bases and prerequisites of a leading nationality are, first, at all hazards, freedom, worldly wealth and products on the largest and most

the most continuous, by understanding well their harmonious relations with entire humanity and history, and all their laws and progress, sublimed with the creative thought of Deity, through all time, past, present, and future. Thus will they expand to the amplitude of their destiny, and become illustrations and culminating parts of the cosmos, and of civilization.

No more considering the States as an incident, or series of incidents, however vast, coming accidentally along the path of time, and shaped by casual emergencies as they happen to rise, and the mere result of modern improvements, vulgar and lucky, ahead of other nations and times, I would finally plant, as seeds, these thoughts or speculations in the growth of our republic—that it is the deliberate culmination and result of all the past—that here, too, as in all departments of the universe, regular laws (slow and sure in planting, slow and sure in ripening) have controll'd and govern'd, and will yet control and govern; and that those laws can no more be baffled or steer'd clear of, or vitiated, by chance, or any fortune or opposition, than the laws of winter and summer, or darkness and light.

The summing up of the tremendous moral and military perturbations of 1861–5, and their results—and indeed of the entire hundred years of the past of our national experiment, from its inchoate movement down to the present day (1780–1881)—is, that they all now launch the United States fairly forth, consistently with the entirety of civilization and humanity, and in main sort the representative of them, leading the van, leading the fleet of the modern and democratic, on the seas and voyages of the future.

And the real history of the United States—starting from that great convulsive struggle for unity, the secession war, triumphantly concluded, and *the South* victorious after all—is only to be written at the remove of hundreds, perhaps a thousand, years hence.

[217]

varied scale, common education and intercom-
munication, and, in general, the passing through
of just the stages and crudities we have passed or
are passing through in the United States.

Then, perhaps, as weightiest factor of the
whole business, and of the main outgrowths of
the future, it remains to be definitely avow'd that
the native-born middle-class population of quite
all the United States—the average of farmers
and mechanics everywhere—the real, though
latent and silent bulk of America, city or country, presents a magnificent mass of material,
never before equaled on earth. It is this material,
quite unexpress'd by literature or art, that in
every respect insures the future of the republic.
During the Secession War I was with the armies,
and saw the rank and file, north and south, and
studied them for four years. I have never had
the least doubt about the country in its essential
future since.

Meantime, we can (perhaps) do no better
than to saturate ourselves with, and continue
to give imitations, yet awhile, of the æsthetic

models, supplies, of that past and of those lands we spring from. Those wondrous stores, reminiscences, floods, currents! Let them flow on, flow hither freely. And let the sources be enlarged, to include not only the works of British origin, as now, but stately and devout Spain, courteous France, profound Germany, the manly Scandinavian lands, Italy's art race, and always the mystic Orient. Remembering that at present, and doubtless long ahead, a certain humility would well become us. The course through time of highest civilization, does it not wait the first glimpse of our contribution to its cosmic train of poems, bibles, first-class structures, perpetuities —Egypt and Palestine and India—Greece and Rome and mediæval Europe—and so onward? The shadowy procession is not a meagre one, and the standard not a low one. All that is mighty in our kind seems to have already trod the road. Ah, never may America forget her thanks and reverence for samples, treasures such as these— that other life-blood, inspiration, sunshine, hourly in use to-day, all days, forever, through her broad demesne!

RIVULETS OF PROSE

All serves our New World progress, even the bafflers, head-winds, cross-tides. Through many perturbations and squalls, and much backing and filling, the ship, upon the whole, makes unmistakably for her destination. Shakspere has served, and serves, may-be, the best of any.

For conclusion, a passing thought, a contrast, of him who, in my opinion, continues and stands for the Shaksperean cultus at the present day among all English-writing peoples—of Tennyson, his poetry. I find it impossible, as I taste the sweetness of those lines, to escape the flavor, the conviction, the lush-ripening culmination, and last honey of decay (I dare not call it rottenness) of that feudalism which the mighty English dramatist painted in all the splendors of its noon and afternoon. And how they are chanted —both poets! Happy those kings and nobles to be so sung, so told! To run their course—to get their deeds and shapes in lasting pigments—the very pomp and dazzle of the sunset!

Meanwhile, democracy waits the coming of its bards in silence and in twilight—but 'tis the twilight of the dawn.

NOTES AND FRAGMENTS

DANTE

From Notes and Fragments, Edited by Dr. Richard Maurice Bucke (London, Ontario, 1899).

THE points of the "Inferno," (I am giving my first impressions,) are *hasting on*, great vigor, a lean muscular ruggedness; no superfluous flesh; and the fascination there always is in a well told tragedy, no matter how painful or repulsive. It signifies, in its way, that melancholy and imperious part of humanity or its elements, out of which the whole structure of the stern and vindictive Jehovahn theology has arisen—from the time of the primitive Jews down—vengeance, gloating in the agony of sinners, bad men, enemies to be punished, and the usual distinctions of good and evil.

It is a short poem. Dante's whole works appear to lie in a very moderate compass. It seems strange that he should stand as the highest type of Italian imaginative art-execution in literature —so gaunt, so haggard and unrich, unjoyous. But the real Italian art-execution flourishes of course in other fields—in music, for instance, peerless in the whole earth, teaching high over the heads of all lands, all times.

Mark the simplicity of Dante, like the Bible's —different from the tangled and florid Shakspere. Some of his idioms must, in Italian, cut like a knife. He narrates like some short-worded, superb illiterate—an old farmer or some New England blue-light minister or common person interested in telling his or her story—makes the impression of *bona fide* in all that he says as if it were certainly so. I do not wonder that the middle ages thought he had indeed really descended into Hell and seen what he described.

Mark, I say, his economy of words—perhaps no other writer ever equal to him. One simple trail of idea, epical, makes the poem—all else resolutely ignored. This alone shows the master. In this respect is the most perfect in all literature. A great study for diffuse moderns.

NOTES AND FRAGMENTS

EMERSON

The superiority of Emerson's writings is in their character—they mean something. He may be obscure but he is certain. Any other of the best American writers has in general a clearer style, has more of the received grace and ease, is less questioned and forbidden than he, makes a handsomer appearance in the society of the books, sells better, passes his time more apparently in the popular understanding; yet there is something in the solitary specimen of New England that outvies them all. He has what none else has; he does what none else does. He pierces the crusts that envelop the secrets of life. He joins on equal terms the few great sages and original seers. He represents the freeman, America, the individual. He represents the gentleman. No teacher or poet of old times or modern times has made a better report of manly and womanly qualities, heroism, chastity, temperance, friendship, fortitude. None has given more beautiful accounts of truth and justice. His words shed light to the best souls; they do not admit of argument. As a sprig from the pine tree or a glimpse anywhere into the daylight belittles all artificial flower work and all the painted scenery of theatres, so are live words in a book compared to cunningly composed words.

A few among men (soon perhaps to become many) will enter easily into Emerson's meanings; by those he will be well-loved. The flippant writer, the orthodox critic, the number of good or indifferent imitators, will not comprehend him; to them he will indeed be a transcendentalist, a writer of sunbeams and moonbeams, a strange and unapproachable person.

Footnote by R. M. Bucke.
Written as a magazine article, date May, 1847. To judge by paper and writing goes back to early fifties. W. (it would seem) knew Emerson pretty well in those early days.

JOHNSON

Samuel Johnson—1709–1784—was born in Litchfield, England. Father a book-seller, educated thoroughly, read everything, went through college, physically queer, scrofulous, purblind, crochety, alimentive, married a vulgar old woman that painted and wore all sorts

[224]

of false things—was faithful and fond to the last—"Dear Titty" went to London, struggled on there thirty years through all sorts of privations and starvations—sometimes lucky (a little) —wrote "Idler," "Rambler," etc.—"Rasselas," written in a week to make money for mother's funeral expenses, etc.,—wrote Dictionary—had £1500 for it—edited an edition of Shakespeare (a poor one) at last received a pension of £300 a year from the Government—was always of coarse behavior,—wrote in a latinized style, not simple and with unlearned instincts but pompous and full of polysyllables.

(Written about 1856.)

A PERFECT SCHOOL

Notes for a poem describing a perfect School. From an unpublished Mss.

GYMNASTIC, moral, mental and sentimental, in which magnificent men are formed.

Old persons come just as much as youth. Gymnastics, physiology, music, swimming bath, conversation, declamation. Large salons adorned with pictures and sculpture. Great ideas, not taught in sermons but imbibed as health is imbibed. Old history taught.

Love—love of women, all manly exercises, rides, rowing.

The greatest persons come.

The President comes, the governors come— political economy.

The American idea in all its amplitude and comprehensiveness.

Grounds, gardens, flowers, grains.

WALT WHITMAN